DATE DUE			
JA 26 '98			

Jean-Paul Sartre

Twayne's World Authors Series

French Literature

David O'Connell, Editor
University of Illinois

JEAN-PAUL SARTRE
(1905–1980)
Photograph by Jacques Robert
Courtesy of *La Nouvelle Revue Française*

Jean-Paul Sartre

By Catharine Savage Brosman

Twayne Publishers • *Boston*

Jean-Paul Sartre

Catharine Savage Brosman

Copyright © 1983 by G.K. Hall & Company
All Rights Reserved
Published by Twayne Publishers
A Division of G. K. Hall & Company
70 Lincoln Street
Boston, Massachusetts 02111

Book Production by Marne B. Sultz

Book Design by Barbara Anderson

Printed on permanent/durable acid-free
paper and bound in the United States of
America.
First Paperback Edition, March 1984

Library of Congress Cataloging in
Publication Data

Brosman, Catharine Savage, 1934–
Jean-Paul Sartre.

(Twayne's world authors series ;
TWAS 697)
Bibliography: p. 133
Includes index.
1. Sartre, Jean-Paul, 1905–1980
—Criticism and interpretation.
I. Title. II. Series.
PQ2637.A82Z59   1983 848'.91409
83-4382
ISBN 0-8057-6544-1 (Hardcover)
ISBN 0-8057-6590-5 (Paperback)

Contents

About the Author

Preface

Acknowledgments

Abbreviations

Chronology

Chapter One
Introduction and Biography   1

Chapter Two
Sartre's Philosophy through 1945:
Phenomenology and Ontology   18

Chapter Three
The Early Fiction   39

Chapter Four
The Later Fiction   55

Chapter Five
The Early Drama   72

Chapter Six
The Later Drama   85

Chapter Seven
Criticism, Biographies, and Late Philosophy   100

Chapter Eight
Conclusion   119

Notes and References   123
Selected Bibliography   133
Index   139

About the Author

Catharine Savage Brosman, who received the Ph.D. in 1960 from Rice University, taught there, at the University of Florida, and at Sweet Briar and Mary Baldwin Colleges before joining in 1968 the faculty of Tulane University, where she is professor of French. She has also served on the faculty of the University of Waterloo, Ontario. She was the recipient of a Fulbright grant and is a member of Phi Beta Kappa. Her scholarly publications include *André Gide: l'évolution de sa pensée religieuse* (1962), *Malraux, Sartre, and Aragon as Political Novelists* (1964), *Roger Martin du Gard* (1968), and numerous articles on nineteenth- and twentieth-century French literature. Her published poetry includes *Watering*, a collection (1972), and poems in leading quarterlies. She is a former president of the South Central Modern Language Association and former managing editor of the *French Review*.

Preface

In view of the existence of numerous critical volumes in English on Jean-Paul Sartre's work already, it may seem needless to offer still another. Unlike early ones, this study has the advantage of being based on Sartre's entire production, excluding posthumous texts, and of taking into account lengthy assessments he made of his own work before he died. It is, moreover, intended to fill a particular need which most existing volumes do not address: that of informing a general audience, especially students and readers in other disciplines, about Sartre's entire career and achievements, in a concise, balanced presentation, clearly organized and easy to consult, and which thus may be useful also to those already familiar with Sartre. It attempts to describe, analyze, and assess, as lucidly as possible and with careful documentation, the chief works of fiction, drama, and criticism in Sartre's canon in relation to his philosophy and its development. I do not offer this study, then, as a new departure in Sartrean criticism, nor should readers expect the application of innovative methodologies, although it takes into account the most recent work on Sartre. While the two aspects of his career are intimately related and there is no wish to imply that one is less important, it is somewhat more concerned with him as a man of letters than as a philosopher. To suggest that he remains more easily accessible to many readers through his fiction and drama than his philosophic and political writings is to recognize what he himself long believed: that literature is action, that it is directed toward an audience, and that its potentiality for touching minds and provoking reactions is unparalleled. Indeed, in his last years he expressed his preference for his literary work over his philosophical endeavors.

I wish to express appreciation to Tulane University for a semester's sabbatical leave that helped me write this book, and to my husband, Paul, my daughter, Kate, and my friends, especially Evelyn and Louise, gratitude for their interest and support.

Catharine Savage Brosman

Tulane University

Acknowledgments

I wish to thank the respective publishers for permission to quote from the following works: Jean-Paul Sartre, *The Words,* trans. Bernard Frechtman, © 1964 by George Braziller, Inc., originally published as *Les Mots,* © 1964 by Librairie Gallimard; Jean-Paul Sartre, *Saint Genet, comédien et martyr,* © 1952 by Librairie Gallimard (special thanks are due to George Braziller, publishers of the American translation, for allowing me to use my own translations); Jean-Paul Sartre, *The Transcendence of the Ego,* trans. F. Williams and R. Kirkpatrick, © 1957 by Farrar, Straus, and Cudahy (permission granted by Farrar, Straus, and Giroux), originally published in *Recherches Philosophiques,* 1937; Simone de Beauvoir, *Memoirs of a Dutiful Daughter,* trans. James Kirkup, © 1974 by Harper and Row Publishers, originally published as *Mémoires d'une jeune fille rangée,* © 1958 by Librairie Gallimard; Jean-Paul Sartre, *The Age of Reason,* trans. Eric Sutton, ©1947 by Alfred A. Knopf, Inc., originally published as *L'Age de raison,* © 1945 by Librairie Gallimard; Jean-Paul Sartre, *The Reprieve,* trans. Eric Sutton, © 1947 by Alfred A. Knopf, Inc., originally published as *Le Sursis,* © 1945 by Librairie Gallimard; Jean-Paul Sartre, *Troubled Sleep,* trans. Eric Sutton, © 1951 by Alfred A. Knopf, Inc., originally published as *La Mort dans l'âme,* © 1949 by Librairie Gallimard; Jean-Paul Sartre, *No Exit and Three Other Plays,* trans. Lionel Abel, © 1955 by Alfred A. Knopf, Inc., originally published as *Huis-clos,* © 1945 by Librairie Gallimard, *Les Mouches,* © 1943 by Librairie Gallimard, *Les Mains sales,* © 1948 by Librairie Gallimard, *La Putain respectueuse,* © 1946 by Nagel; Jean-Paul Sartre, *The Condemned of Altona,* trans. S. and G. Leeson, © 1961 by Alfred A. Knopf, Inc., originally published as *Les Séquestrés d'Altona,* © 1960 by Librairie Gallimard; Jean-Paul Sartre, *The Devil and the Good Lord and Two Other Plays,* trans. Kitty Black and S. and G. Leeson, © 1960 by Alfred A. Knopf, Inc., originally published as *Le Diable et le Bon Dieu,* © 1951 by Librairie Gallimard, *Kean,* © 1954 by Librairie Gallimard, *Nekrassov,* © 1956 by Librairie Gallimard; Jean-Paul Sartre, *The Trojan Women,* adap. Ronald Duncan, © 1967 by Alfred A. Knopf, Inc., originally published as *Les Troyennes,* © 1966 by Librairie Gallimard; Jean-Paul Sartre, *The Wall,* trans. Lloyd Alexander, copyright 1948 by New Directions Publishing Corp., Copyright © 1975 by Lloyd Alexander, reprinted by permission of New Directions Publishing Corp., originally published as *Le Mur,* © 1939 by Librairie Gallimard; Jean-Paul Sartre, *Nausea,* trans. Lloyd Alexander, Copyright © 1964 by New Directions Publishing Corp., All rights reserved.

Abbreviations

The following abbreviations will be used in the text and notes for works referred to repeatedly. Complete bibliographical information is given in the bibliography. Other parenthetical in-text references will be to the work under consideration, as indicated in the notes.

BN   Jean-Paul Sartre, *Being and Nothingness*

C   Simone de Beauvoir, *La Cérémonie des adieux*

CRD   Jean-Paul Sartre, *Critique de la raison dialectique*

FC   Simone de Beauvoir, *The Force of Circumstance*

MD   Simone de Beauvoir, *Memoirs of a Dutiful Daughter*

PL   Simone de Beauvoir, *The Prime of Life*

S   Jean-Paul Sartre, *Situations*, vols. I-X

SH   Jean-Paul Sartre, *Sartre by Himself*

SV   Francis Jeanson, *Sartre dans sa vie*

TCF   Simone de Beauvoir, *Tout Compte fait*

TS   Jean-Paul Sartre, *Un Théâtre de situations*

W   Jean-Paul Sartre, *The Words*

WS   Michel Contat and Michel Rybalka, *The Writings of Jean-Paul Sartre*, vol. I, *A Bibliographical Life*

Chronology

1905   Jean-Paul Sartre born in Paris on 21 June.

1906   Death of Sartre's father.

1915   After tutoring and irregular schooling, enters the Lycée Henri IV; meets Paul Nizan.

1917   Moves to La Rochelle with mother and her new husband.

1920   Returns to Lycée Henri IV in Paris, as boarding pupil.

1921   Passes first baccalaureate examination.

1922   Passes second baccalaureate examination.

1924   Enters Ecole Normale Supérieure.

1927   *Diplôme d'études supérieures.*

1929   Meets Simone de Beauvoir; passes examination for the *agrégation* in philosophy, after failing the year before.

1929–1931   Military service.

1931   First teaching post, spring, at Le Havre; publication of a short story in a minor periodical.

1933–1934   Studies at the Institut Français in Berlin; reads phenomenology and works on *La Nausée.*

1934–1939   Teaching posts in various cities in the provinces and outskirts of Paris; summertime travels with Beauvoir.

1936–1937   First philosophic essays published.

1938   *La Nausée* (first novel) published.

1939   *Le Mur* (short stories) published, and additional publications in philosophy; also critical articles.

1939–1940   Mobilization and service in the meteorological section, near the German border; captured on 21 June and imprisoned in France and Germany.

1941   Return from Germany, March; settles in Paris.

1943   *L'Etre et le néant* (major ontological study) and *Les Mouches* (play); meets Camus; writes filmscripts.

1944   *Huis-clos* (play).

1945   *L'Age de raison* and *Le Sursis* (novels); first issue of the monthly, *Les Temps Modernes;* first trip to the United States (henceforth, frequent travels in Europe and to other continents, many in Beauvoir's company); lecture, "L'Existentialisme est un humanisme."

1946   *Morts sans sépulture* and *La Putain respectueuse* (plays); great popularity in Paris and fame as an existentialist.

1947   Essay on Baudelaire; publication of *Situations* I.

1948   Joins Rassemblement Démocratique Révolutionnaire, a political movement, which he leaves the next year; *Les Mains sales* (play); *Situations* II ("Qu'est-ce que la littérature?").

1949   *La Mort dans l'âme* (novel).

1951   *Le Diable et le Bon Dieu* (play).

1952   *Saint Genet, comédien et martyr* (criticism); draws close to the French Communists and writes essay on Cold War; quarrel with Camus.

1953   Begins autobiography; goes through serious intellectual crisis and reevaluation of his career; spends much of the summer in Rome, as he will do during most of the following summers, up to his death.

1954   First trip to the USSR; hospitalization.

1955   Trip to China and the USSR.

1956   Criticizes Soviet invasion of Hungary.

1957   Criticizes Algerian policy of French government; intense activity, with the use of stimulants.

1958   Criticizes De Gaulle and campaigns against ratification of the constitution of the Fifth Republic.

1959   *Les Séquestrés d'Altona* (play); fatigue and ill health.

1960   *Critique de la raison dialectique* (Marxist-existentialist essay on history and groups); long stay in Brazil and visit to Cuba; support of Algerian nationalists.

1964   *Les Mots* (autobiography); refuses Nobel Prize.

1965   Officially adopts a girl from Algeria.

1966   Lectures in Japan.

1967   Visits Egypt and Israel; presides over Russell War Crimes Tribunal.

1968   Actively supports students in the May uprisings; association with Maoist groups; condemns Soviet invasion of Czechoslovakia, which he had visited in 1963.

1969   Death of Sartre's mother; countless protests and interventions on behalf of social and political groups and causes, almost until the end of his life.

1971–1972   *L'Idiot de la famille* (on Flaubert).

1973   Loss of sight so great that he cannot read and thus ceases writing; circulatory troubles; travels frequently, however, and maintains contact with friends, young people, and political groups.

1974   Interviews with Simone de Beauvoir, in lieu of continuing his autobiography.

1975   Important interview with Michel Contat in *Le Nouvel Observateur,* translated in *New York Review of Books* and reprinted in *Situations* X.

1977   Publication of a long fragment of the second volume of the *Critique* in *New Left Review.*

1980   During last illness, cared for by close friends, including Beauvoir; death on 15 April.

Chapter One
Introduction and Biography

Jean-Paul Sartre is surely one of the major intellectual figures of his century. Michel Contat and Michel Rybalka, his bibliographers, call him "uncontestably the most outstanding philosopher and writer of our time" (*WS*, xiii). Although appreciations of his philosophical and literary work vary, and his credit may rise or fall in the future according to the reigning political ideologies, it is hard to imagine an evaluation of intellectual life in Europe in the twentieth century that would not grant him a prominent place. Endowed with a fine analytical mind, a considerable literary talent—including an ear for speech—a taste for philosophical problems, and abundant energy, he was granted both the long life and the circumstances in which to develop and display these qualities to advantage in more than thirty volumes of fiction, drama, philosophy, criticism, essays, and polemics, as well as countless articles. His increasingly radical and active political stance in the last third of his life, while shedding a critical light on some of his earlier attitudes and accomplishments and helping bring about his farewell to imaginative literature, enriched his work in new ways and added to the complexity of his positions and to his influence. Though detractors may find fault with his works, ideas, and political positions, the legacy Sartre leaves to readers in the 1980s and beyond is that of a powerful critical intellect, confronting many of the major issues of his time and giving to this confrontation inventive and striking expressions.

Childhood and Youth

Sartre was born in Paris on 21 June 1905, the only son of a naval engineer, Jean-Baptiste Sartre, and his wife, Anne-Marie, née Schweitzer.[1] The only surviving daughter and youngest child of Charles Schweitzer, a language teacher from Alsace, Anne-Marie was the first cousin of Albert Schweitzer (son of Charles's brother Louis). Sartre's

1

paternal grandfather, a country doctor from Périgord, is said never again to have addressed a word to his wife after learning, following the wedding, that her father, far from being wealthy, was ruined; nevertheless he begot three children. On 17 September 1906, Sartre's father died of fever he had contracted in Indochina. Shortly thereafter, the young widow and her son returned to live with her parents, first in Meudon, then (1911) in Paris. Sartre treats the death of his father as a fortunate event, which gave him his liberty (from a paternal model and authority, or, in Freudian terms, from a superego), although it sent his mother "back to her chains" (*W*, 11).[2] He compares this event to another, his weaning at the age of nine months, when Anne-Marie had to give him to a nurse so that she might attend to her sick husband; this, he said, was traumatic, whereas he was not even aware of the loss of his father. Although some critics have asserted that standards he endorsed later imply that he thought it would have been preferable to grow up with a father, in a normal family, he generally appears grateful this was not the case.[3] Instead, he and his young mother—jointly called "the children"—were for several years under the tutelage of Charles Schweitzer (and to a lesser degree of the grandmother, Louise), in an unusual situation to which he attributes great importance. This upbringing, which contributed to his caustic portraits of the bourgeoisie, deserves further attention.

While Charles, a severe, domineering, formidable old Protestant, who sometimes took himself for Victor Hugo, sometimes for God the Father (*W*, 14–15), incarnated a stern idea of morality—and there is no doubt that Sartre's convictions and attitudes are often very Puritanical in flavor—he viewed his grandson as a marvel, a diversion for his old age and guarantee of biological immortality, lavished attention on him, and treated him indulgently (*C*, 327). Inclined toward role-playing, he unconsciously taught it to the boy, who later discovered and turned away from this family comedy. Charles was preeminently a believer in words (whence the title of Sartre's autobiography) as expressions of truth and beauty as well as a livelihood; he conveyed to the boy a strong love of books and everything that appeals to the imagination, a cult which came from a nineteenth-century progressive conviction about the value of learning for both the individual and society. Jean-Paul, who taught himself to read at a very early age, had few contacts with other children, engaged little in outdoor play and sport, and found his entertainment chiefly in reading. He attempted to write novels; he indulged also in imaginary adventures, based on classics such as *Don Quixote* and children's books, in which he played heroic roles. Until he was ten, this penchant for the imaginary was not counteracted by the real world of school and friends, since Charles kept him at home and, with few exceptions, was his only tutor. Only short stays at the grammar school at Arcachon, the Lycée Montaigne, and a small private institution in Paris gave him an experience of group schooling.

Ironically, it was, according to Sartre, Charles's warnings *against* literature as a career which confirmed his image of himself as a writer, and thus were responsible for his long literary career. *Les Mots (The Words)* can be seen as the history and analysis of a vocation, like Proust's great novel, except that Sartre is hostile to his choice, whereas for Proust art represented salvation. Not surprisingly, the very middle-class grandfather, while looking with reverence upon the written word and cultivating an aesthetic approach to his own activities, had thoroughly conventional reactions to the prospect that his grandson should take up writing seriously. Warning him that he must adopt also a remunerative profession such as teaching, he mentioned Jean-Paul's inclination as if it were already a lifetime choice; this was responsible, Sartre says, for turning it into one (*W,* 96–101; *SH,* 6). So that, as a mere boy, Sartre found that an image of himself, a way of being, was chosen for him. This interpretation of his childhood, while questionable on theoretical grounds, probably does express accurately a subjective feeling of "being" a writer which was at the basis of his career at least until the 1950s. It is also roughly consistent with his analyses of the "original choices" made by Baudelaire, Genet, and Flaubert, whose entire lives were dictated by an early image of themselves.

This discovery of what he would be gave to his youth and most of his maturity direction and confidence. He saw that he was "called" to be great; like Gide, he felt both predestination and justification. "I had the certainty of being elected" (*SV,* 61). The effect was all the greater because, in spite of family doting, he had earlier felt acutely his lack of justification—a feeling which is connected to his views on human contingency and freedom. Life became teleological, that is, with an end. He spoke later of his neurosis, "the notion that since reality had been given to me through books, I would make contact with reality, and offer a more profound truth about the world, if I wrote books myself" (*SH,* 14, 88). But he considered his choice deeper than a neurosis. "One gets rid of a neurosis, one doesn't get cured of oneself" (*W,* 159). Typically, he wished to accept responsibility for this choice, even though his grandfather had provoked it (*W,* 147).

Jean-Paul was of slight build; he was sometimes dressed like a girl, and generally treated as delicate; he had long hair until he was seven. In addition, he suffered from leucoma in his right eye, which led to loss of sight in that eye and a squinting appearance. He was not a pretty child or, later, a handsome man. "I did not feel comfortable in my skin."[4] It is a wonder that these physical factors, as well as lack of playmates, did not create a highly unbalanced person; what is known of his personal life as an adult suggests a relatively well-adjusted, stable, and happy man, if somewhat hostile (C, 368). Perhaps this is because he denied his childhood as much as possible; it may be also because many of the peculiar outlooks nurtured by his odd childhood and unimposing physique were syphoned into his writing. If this is true, art was like a second experience, attached to his deepest self and expressing it, as had his childhood fantasies; it was both Stendhalian compensation and Gidean catharsis, the expression of potentialities of which he rid himself.

The boy's religious training was conflicting. Officially he was Catholic, and he attended catechism classes, though his Catholic grandmother's outlook was skeptical instead of pious. His grandfather's Protestant ties and anticlericalism, however, taught him to mistrust those called Papists. And for none of Sartre's elders did God seem to be more than a shadowy figure, a witness. They were "borderline believers" (SH, 16). His own analysis of his childhood religious situation is that, needing God, belief in whom could have furnished him with a sense of justification and direction, he encountered only the distant pseudo-Deity of official religion, qualified by the opposing viewpoints of his grandparents. "I was led to disbelief not by the conflict of dogmas, but by my grandparents' indifference" (W, 63). Though practicing, he found religion less and less real. Finally, realizing that God's omniscience made him a constant observer and judge of human actions, Sartre rejected this divine presence or gaze as inadmissible; by the time he was in his teens, he was a thorough atheist, a position from which he never departed.[5] In 1951 he said he was certain God did not exist (SV, 280). Literature afforded him, he later realized, a ready substitute for the lost absolute of faith. "Writing was . . . the equivalent of religion. Theological significance of the literary act" (SV, 21). If disbelief in God came easily, disbelief in literature as sacred came less so. Only many years later could he say that he believed he had carried out the "cruel and long-range affair" of total atheism (W, 158).

At the age of ten, Sartre entered the Lycée Henri IV in Paris, and, after a period of adjustment, performed well, made friends, and fit well into the games. When he was eleven, his mother remarried and in the autumn of 1917 he joined his family in La Rochelle, where his stepfather, Joseph Mancy, was director of a shipyard. In view of his stress on the remarriage of Baudelaire's mother, which provoked his jealousy and imposed a detested authority figure, it is inviting to speculate on the relationships in the new household. Sometimes Sartre spoke of his stepfather with respect, and affirmed that as a boy he felt no jealousy toward him.[6] Yet there are many unfavorable glimpses of him in Sartre's writings; the two were temperamentally very different. Beauvoir calls him authoritarian and demanding (*TCF*, 104), and commentators generally believe that the boy felt betrayed and even loathed his stepfather.[7] The adjustment thus appears to have been difficult, as was the move to the lycée of La Rochelle, where his classmates were hostile to him and he performed indifferently for some time (*C*, 192–93; *SV*, 291; *SH*, 10). Sartre called the years 1917 to 1920 the three or four worst years of his life (*SV*, 43).

Young Manhood

In 1920, Sartre returned to Paris as a boarding pupil at the Lycée Henri IV. Performing well, he passed his baccalaureate exams in 1921 and 1922 and prepared at Louis-le-Grand for the entrance examinations to the Ecole Normale Supérieure, which he passed in 1924. He received several certificates and did his *diplôme d'études supérieures*, with a thesis on images, in 1927 (*SV*, 46, 293). He had at first found philosophy uninspiring (*S* IX, 13), but, under the guidance of a lycée professor whom he liked, and later as a university student reading Bergson, he discovered with delight that philosophy was both a body of truth and a way toward truth, and he took courses in psychology and philosophy to prepare for a teaching career, while remaining convinced that he would also be a writer (*C*, 177; *SH*, 27–28). Although his published autobiography ends when he is still a child, since his life had been determined by then,[8] the memoirs of Simone de Beauvoir, his friend and then intimate companion from his last university months (July 1929) (*SV*, 52), give abundant glimpses of him as a student, and then follow his career insofar as it was closely associated with her own. She portrays him as an attractively eccentric and brilliant youth, a lively conversationalist, with a good voice and undeniable comic talents, said by his friends to think all the time except when he was asleep (*SH*, 22–23; *MD*, 337). "He was a sort of intellectual revolutionary, before whom no sentiment, no value, no moral concern was acceptable: a man of refusal and condemnation" (*SV*, 53).

Philosophic training in France in the 1920s was dominated by a parochial idealism, to which Sartre reacted negatively (*C*, 205). At the Lycée Henri IV, Alain taught his own variety. At the university, great modern names such as Hegel, Marx, Nietzsche, and Husserl were not commented on; only in 1933 did Sartre become acquainted with Husserl.[9] Among philosophers he read in the late 1920s are Leibniz and Karl Jaspers, whose treatise on psychopathology he helped translate and proof-read (*WS,* 6; *PL,* 39). He read Freud, whose influence penetrated very slowly into France, but rejected his theses (*S* IX, 104). His first reading of Marx had little influence on him (*C,* 481). In literature, he was acquainted with surrealism and the principal moderns—Proust (probably the one who influenced him the most), Giraudoux, Morand, Valéry, Gide, whom he says he did not like much (*SH,* 19) but to whom he probably owes a considerable debt, in addition to Dostoyevsky, Joyce, and others (*C,* 24–49). He stressed that he was of the generation whose intellectual masters were Gide and Proust, an age of subjectivism and idealism (*SV,* 24). He credits his close friend and classmate, Paul Nizan, a promising writer who became a fervent Communist, with bringing several authors to his attention.[10] The influence of surrealism and Proust (who taught him about social milieux) is especially visible in his first novel, and much of Sartrean reflection on consciousness bears comparison to Valéry's thought. Beauvoir pointed out, however, that Sartre's literary tastes always included popular types such as detective and serialized novels, and he said he preferred thrillers to Wittgenstein (*W,* 48; *SH,* 17). Like them, his own works are often characterized by melodramatic situations and popular speech. He also liked jazz, Negro spirituals, and other popular American music (*MD,* 335). Above all, he lived to *write,* not to be a philosopher (*S* IX, 13; *C,* 200–205); philosophic disputes made him "shrug his shoulders," and Beauvoir found him totally committed to literature, though he once said he wished to be *both* Stendhal and Spinoza (*C,* 166). "The work of art or literature was, in his view, an absolute end in itself; and it was even . . . the be-all and end-all of the entire universe" (*MD,* 341).

In 1928 Sartre failed the written examination for the *agrégation,* perhaps because he treated the topic, contingency, in a novel fashion (*SV,* 294–95); a year later, he passed first in the class. Between November 1929 and February 1931 he did his military service—somewhat reluctantly, despite generous leaves—in the meteorological section, first at Fort Saint-Cyr, near Versailles, then at Saint-Symphorien, near Tours. Upon returning in 1931, he was not appointed, as he had hoped, to a lectureship in Japan, but instead became professor of philosophy at the lycée in Le Havre (*PL,* 65). He spent the academic year 1933–34 in Berlin at the Institut Français, reading German phenomenologists and writing. After two more years at Le Havre, he taught at Laon (1936–37), refusing a better post at Lyons so that he could be near Beauvoir and would be more likely to be transferred to Paris, then was appointed to the Lycée Pasteur in Neuilly (1937–39, spring 1941), later to the Lycée Condorcet (1941–44), his last post. He and Beauvoir, who was to be his lifetime, though not exclusive, companion, declined to marry, since they did not want children, and marriage ran counter to their ideas of personal independence; Sartre did not want to give up, she said, "contingent" loves.[11]

Before Sartre's literary career in the 1930s is traced, it is worthwhile glancing at his activities up to the mobilization of September 1939. He was an extremely outgoing person, naturally cheerful, who spent a great deal of time with friends. He was interested in his students, whom he treated more like fellow-learners than subordinates. In 1935–36, he and Beauvoir became so friendly with a young woman, Olga Kosakiewicz, that they added her to their couple and became a trio—an ultimately unsuccessful experiment. Sartre did not care for nature or outdoor activity, though he did accompany Beauvoir on numerous excursions on foot. He was fond of games and of the cinema, on which he lectured in 1931 and which he placed very high in aesthetic ranking; he even helped make some amateur movies. Beauvoir's memoirs and his work give evidence of his enormously wide reading in literature, philosophy, and psychology: Freud, Claudel, Saint-Exupéry, Malraux, Morand, Céline (an important influence), Sinclair Lewis, Dos Passos, Hemingway, Faulkner, D. H. Lawrence, Kafka, Trotsky, and some Heidegger, which at first he did not understand. He traveled frequently, taking long vacation trips in many European countries, usually in Beauvoir's company.

Sartre's political views were radical, at least in comparison to the bourgeois republicanism of his family (see *C,* 473 ff.). He was strongly anticapitalist, antielitist, and proworker; without knowing Marxism well, he accepted in general Marxist analyses of economics and history, while refusing to deny importance to the bourgeois intellectual. He applauded the victory of the Popular Front in 1936 and disapproved of Fascism in Germany, Italy, and Spain (*C,* 447–48). But he was far from being an activist or even a dogmatic socialist, since socialism implied bureaucratic organization, which would probably exclude writers. He was more of an anarchist than a revolutionary. Like much of the Left around 1930, he felt that capitalist institutions were so bankrupt that they would crumble and burn by themselves, and that a new society would be born from their ashes. Meanwhile, he had society to criticize, as a kind of foil for his "opposition aesthetics" (*MD,* 342). During the 1930s he remained politically inactive, not voting and often not reading the newspapers, tied to his class, the petty bourgeoisie, not only by his mode of living—a civil servant's—but by his attitudes. Only occasionally did he consider joining the Communist party (*PL,* 111). His position is to be contrasted with that of many other French intellectuals, such as Gide, Malraux, and Nizan, who in the 1930s took public political stands. For him, history continued to be a backdrop for his personal and literary life, and only through his teaching and writing did he wish to participate in changing society. Characteristically, he felt totally free of social and political forces, a position that would change with the war. It is, wrote Francis Jeanson, as if "he had above all proposed to pursue a strictly personal adventure, to develop his aptitudes, his knowledge, and his concrete experience of reality, *at the expense of any commitment of a political or historical nature*" (*SV,* 69; Jeanson's emphasis). At the time of the Spanish Civil War, "a drama that for the next two and a half years was to dominate our lives" (*PL,* 220), Sartre did not consider participating, but was in favor of the Republicans and, like many Europeans, thought that the struggle was a threat to all Europe, a sign of conflicts to come between Fascism and the democracies (*PL,* 221). He judged the Munich pact foolish, since ultimately Hitler would have to be restrained (*PL,* 268).

Sartre's literary career began when, as a student, he contributed to and acted in a student revue (*C,* 237), wrote two novels (mostly unpublished), a story (which appeared in 1923), an essay (published) on the theory of the state in French thought (*SV,* 46), and other pieces. During his military service he tried his hand at poetry, a novel fragment, a drama, and essays, a fragment of which appeared as "La Légende de la vérité" ("The Legend of Truth") in the review *Bifur* in 1931. The latter, Beauvoir recalls, was an attempt to express his developing ideas in concrete terms—a characteristic position throughout his career. The manuscript of essays was rejected for publication and he put it away, writing meanwhile the "pamphlet on contingency" which became *La Nausée (Nausea).* During the following years he worked on it and his first philosophical treatises, *L'Imagination (Imagination)* (1936) and "La Transcendance de l'ego" (*The Transcendence of the Ego*) (1937). In 1935 he took mescaline as an experiment in imagination; after months of depression, during which he had various animal fantasies (especially crabs and lobsters) which revealed his apprehension of nature, his hallucinations ceased.

In 1937, *La Nausée* was accepted by Gallimard; in 1936 and 1937 Sartre composed stories, some of which appeared in important French reviews. He worked on "La Psyché," part of which became *Esquisse d'une théorie des émotions (The Emotions)* (1939). In 1938 he composed "L'Enfance d'un chef" ("The Childhood of a Leader") and began another novel; *La*

Nausée (1938) and his stories, published in 1939 under the title *Le Mur (The Wall)*, were well received.

Wartime and Immediate Postwar Period

When the Second World War began in September 1939, Sartre was still primarily a professor of philosophy, secondarily a writer; though he was known in the intellectual circles of the *NRF* and Gallimard, he by no means had national fame. After having spent the last prewar weeks vacationing, he was called up immediately for service in the meteorological section, where his duties were not onerous. In November Beauvoir visited him in Alsace, and in February and April 1940 he had furloughs in Paris. His *L'Imaginaire (Psychology of the Imagination)* was published the same spring. On 21 June he was captured by the Germans, without having been involved in fighting, and was interned, first in France, then in Germany, until March 1941. This experience of imprisonment was relatively benign; he had no acquaintance with the torture, starvation, and genocide which writers such as Jean Cayrol witnessed, which colored all their postwar work. But in close proximity with others, Sartre discovered a different way of seeing the world, essentially one of fraternity, solidarity, and a "unanimous life" (*S* IV, 349; X, 180). For the first time, he knew well men from the working and peasant classes, with whom he discovered much in common, and also became acquainted with several priests, with one of whom in particular he discussed philosophy, especially Heidegger.[12] The idea of freedom, already important to him, took on a concrete meaning and moved to the forefront of his thought, along with the notion of commitment. At Christmas 1940 he produced and acted in a play, one of several he composed in the camp, entitled *Bariona,* on the subject of Roman-occupied Palestine at the time of Christ's birth. In March, he was repatriated as a civilian, having falsified his military papers to indicate unfitness for service and thus convince the Germans that he was not a conscript (showing them also, as proof, his bad eye) (*PL,* 381). He soon finished the first novel of his series, *Les Chemins de la liberté (The Roads to Freedom),* and resumed his lycée duties, until, in 1944, he asked to be put on permanent leave, though he liked teaching (*S* X, 177).

The four years between 1941 and 1945 were extremely productive for him, and also laid the foundation for his postwar popularity and intellectual leadership. He made many acquaintances, including numerous young people who contributed to his lionization after the war; among his friends were Maurice Merleau-Ponty, Alberto Giacometti, Boris Vian, Jean

Genet, Michel Leiris, Arthur Koestler, and Picasso (see *C,* 341–53). He
and Beauvoir did much of their writing and socializing at the Café de
Flore, which was heated. They spent time in the country with friends and
took numerous trips within France in both the occupied and unoccupied
zones, by train and bicycle; meager diet and poor tires were usually their
only difficulties. Sartre lectured on the history of the theater for Charles
Dullin at L'Atelier and wrote scripts for Pathé films. He had returned from
prison camp awakened to his own historicity, obsessed with the idea of
commitment, and believing that a widespread resistance could be easily
organized (a belief he later qualified as naive) (*SH,* 50). Even before the fall
of France, he had decided to become involved in politics when the war
ended (*PL,* 342), feeling that action and commitment were the necessary
corollary of any authentic philosophic and political position. The experience of imprisonment strengthened this attitude; Beauvoir wrote that he
returned a changed man, aware of the limits placed on freedom by
circumstances, committed for the first time not just to criticizing
capitalist and bourgeois society but to participating in the creation of a
new order, which would be essentially socialist (*FC,* 5–6). Never in the
forefront of an important Resistance organization, he nonetheless did
participate in some clandestine activity, first with his own shortlived
movement, Socialisme et Liberté (organized with Merleau-Ponty), then
with several committees of anticollaborationist writers; and, through
Camus, who introduced himself at the premiere of *Les Mouches (The Flies)*
in 1943, he was in touch with Combat, a major group. Though he tried in
1941 to establish contacts between his own group and the Communists,
the latter would not cooperate and spread the rumor that he had been
repatriated to act as an *agent provocateur.* During this period he composed
and published, in addition to many articles, several of his most famous
works, including *L'Etre et le néant (Being and Nothingness).*

The immediate postwar years in France were a time of economic
difficulty, extremely complicated politics, and, for Sartre, great personal
success. It is difficult to convey briefly the complexity of politics then and
of his own positions, which evolved slowly but were sensitive to shifts in
power and attitude among the major political groups. His stance was,
roughly, non-Stalinist communism—a position difficult to maintain both
practically and theoretically. After the Liberation of Paris in August 1944,
a powerful, euphoric optimism made the various Resistance groups believe that their union against the occupant could be maintained as the basis
for constructing a new France, essentially revolutionary. Although this
illusion was shortly dispelled, many leftists continued to seek close

collaboration among Socialists, Communists, and the unaligned Left. For several years Sartre's efforts were directed toward this end. In 1944, with Merleau-Ponty and others, he founded *Les Temps Modernes* (Modern times), named after Chaplin's film, a review intended to bring into focus current questions, chiefly through Marxist lenses; its first number appeared in October 1945. For virtually the rest of his life he remained a chief figure on its editorial board. He denounced the warfare in Indochina as early as 1947 (*FC*, 169–70), and in 1948 supported the creation of the state of Israel. Briefly he and several colleagues had a radio program, during which he attacked the Gaullists and urged close collaboration with the Communists, to whom, however, he was anathema for his lack of orthodoxy, in spite of resemblances in their positions (*SV*, 168; *C*, 354). He said that the Communists' hatred of him made him grow more conscious of his own objectivity for others and the necessity of proving he was right (*FC*, 147–48). He was moderately close to Camus and wrote some in the newspaper *Combat;* but differences of temperament as well as of ideology gradually eroded their friendship, and before the definitive break in 1952 a quarrel kept them apart for several months in 1946–47.[13]

Meanwhile, the publication of *Les Chemins de la liberté* in 1945 and 1949 and the creation of several plays, as well as his journalistic activity and essays, kept Sartre's increasingly prestigious name before the public and gave literary expression to some of his political ideas, even though none of these works is exclusively political. In 1945 his public lecture, "L'Existentialisme est un humanisme" (*Existentialism*), before an overflowing hall, gave publicity to some of his most basic philosophic notions. When the term *existentialist,* which neither he nor Beauvoir had first adopted but which had been attached to them after Gabriel Marcel suggested it (*FC*, 38), became applied, quite erroneously, to a style of conduct, manner of dress, and group of night clubs on the Left Bank, Sartre's notoriety was complete (*SH*, 72–73). It was not an entirely satisfactory recognition. In 1948, the whole of his work was placed by the Holy Office on the Index. He was widely criticized on both left and right; his writings were read much less than they were attacked. As Beauvoir points out (*FC*, 40–41), he had achieved great fame in his middle years, a fame he had originally supposed would be only posthumous, and he had to reconsider his goals in light of this success, which may have been partly responsible for his move toward radicalization.

Sartre traveled considerably after the Liberation, first as a correspondent to America (January-May 1945), then again to the United States for a series of lectures, then, often in Beauvoir's company, to several European countries, Algeria, Central America, Haiti, and Cuba (1949). In America he formed a sentimental attachment which may have briefly threatened his association with Beauvoir but did not ultimately destroy it; with interruptions necessitated by distance, this liaison lasted several years. In 1948 he became involved in a non-Communist, neutralist political movement, the Rassemblement Démocratique Révolutionnaire; by this action, which he considered consistent with his ideological position (*FC*, 147), he hoped to prove that an unaligned Marxist political platform was tenable and to help construct a new, free Europe, independent of both Russian and American influence, at a time when the United States was greatly feared because of its role in the Cold War, rearmament, and McCarthyism. But he resigned in October 1949, disagreeing with the reformist nature of the movement and realizing that this middle position would remain unpopular and thus ineffective (*C*, 460–61; *SV*, 179). Attacked for his philosophic and political ideas, Sartre, putting aside his literary work and political action, began a reconsideration of his positions.

The Fifties

The first years of the decade, characterized by a somber international outlook under the threat of atomic war, were a major turning point in Sartre's career, in which he abandoned idealism, moved toward Marxism, and began his self-radicalization. One cause of his reorientation was his isolation (*C*, 499–500). He felt that his future writings were destined to have few readers, since the audience he wanted—the proletariat—was separated from him by his status as a bourgeois; as he said, he was a contradiction insofar as, a product of the bourgeoisie, he wrote in language the middle classes would understand, about topics of interest to them, and yet hoped the workers would overthrow them (*SH*, 3–4). Moreover, failure to make his unaligned political position widely accepted led him to see that he had to change his tactics. If it was impractical, he had to accept either the American influence or the Soviet, and, unlike Merleau-Ponty, who approved the American action in Korea, he preferred the latter. He had also moved ideologically closer to Marxism as he came to recognize that economic and political conditions are more than elements of a situation, that they fashion and limit freedom (*FC*, 199). "I discovered abruptly that alienation, exploitation of man by man, undernourishment, relegated to the background metaphysical evil, which is a luxury" (*SV*, 227). A product of this shift in his position is his important article of 1952 on Communists and peace (*S* VI), written after the visit of General Ridgway to Paris and the unprovoked arrest of a Communist (*C*, 461). He rejected the non-Communist left as contradictory and effected a *rapprochement* with the Communist party, which accepted him in a quasi-official way, although in 1950 he had criticized the Soviet labor camps. His reading of Henri Guillemin's book on Louis Napoleon was a major factor in his increasing radicalization, since it led him to view the bourgeoisie as an oppressor class, whatever virtues individual members might have (*SH*, 71–72). Similarly, his attitude toward psychoanalysis had changed: whereas during the 1930s he had been unfavorably disposed toward Freudian theory, he now reached the conclusion that, while freedom is always an ontological given, in practice it is limited by one's psychological data, as these develop from early childhood choices. These new convictions led him to believe that increased action was necessary in the struggle against psychological and economic determinism, so that freedom could be realized for all. Having already espoused in "Qu'est-ce que la littérature?" (1947) (*What is Literature?*) writing as action, effecting concrete changes in the present, he grew to believe that greater personal commitment was imperative. The rest of his career was marked by fervent dedication to the causes he found just.

This led to the revision of two other views he had long held. One was that of literature as an absolute (see *C*, 278–79). This notion had already been eroded somewhat in his criticism, but the rejection of aesthetic values was gradual. By 1949, his career as a novelist was over; likewise, most of his drama dates from the earlier period. Increasingly, he came to view literature as an escape, a bourgeois idol, proposing aesthetic pleasure as a false absolute and pseudojustification to both writer and reader. (See, however, *C*, 217.) With this change came a second, in his attitude toward himself. *Les Mots*, conceived in 1953, composed mainly in 1954, finished ten years later, analyzes the sources of his erroneous belief in literature as justification. Though he continued to write essays, plays, and screenplays, his interest was primarily in revising his thought and in political activism. He abandoned his study on ethics, planned since 1943, which he later condemned as "mystified" (*C*, 41). His philosophic investigations in a Marxist vein led in 1960 to the *Critique de la raison dialectique* (the introductory part of which, "Questions de méthode," was translated as *Search for a Method*, the rest as *Critique of Dialectical Reason*). Numerous other texts attest to the intensity of his thought during the remainder of his life. But his most fertile years of literary creation were ended by the crisis of the 1950s.

Sartre continued to travel extensively; from 1953 on he spent almost every summer in Rome. Although he had no taste for luxury, his political convictions did not deter him from using his royalties, like others of the privileged classes.[14] Many of his trips were made with Beauvoir, others with another woman, still others as part of a trio or quartet. (His relationship with Beauvoir had evolved from a liaison into a solid, domesticated friendship.) In 1954 he made a lengthy, if closely supervised, visit in Russia (during which he was hospitalized for high blood pressure and exhaustion from overwork), followed by a two-month trip to China the next year. He composed *Le Diable et le Bon Dieu (The Devil and the Good Lord)* (1951), his study of Jean Genet, and his plays *Kean, Nekrassov,* and *Les Séquestrés d'Altona (The Condemned of Altona,* or *Loser Wins)* (1959).

In addition to increasing closeness to the Communists, 1952 was marked by the public quarrel between Sartre and Camus, after Francis Jeanson had reviewed *L'Homme révolté (The Rebel)* unfavorably in *Les Temps Modernes* and Camus had replied. Sartre's hatred of the bourgeoisie and the United States clashed with what he saw as Camus's increasingly anti-Soviet, humanistic, and idealistic position. His views also diverged from those of Merleau-Ponty, decreasingly Marxist, who in 1955 published a criticism of Sartre's positions, to which Beauvoir replied in Sartre's defense. In 1956 he condemned the Soviet intervention in Hungary, but again drew close to the Communists with the creation of the Fifth Republic. He protested both in the press and through demonstrations against the Gaullist government, which to him was the final step in the movement of French society toward Fascism and its complete ruin (*SH,* 84–85). He concluded that the French Left was powerless to act as a whole against policies in Algeria, and that action by small rebel groups and individuals was imperative.[15] He objected especially to the use of torture by French troops and police, and generally to the continued French presence in North Africa, just as he had disapproved of the French presence in Indochina. He thus came to understand those who actively supported the Algerian rebels.[16] In 1957 he testified for the defense in the trial of an Algerian accused of assassinating a political figure; in 1958 he wrote a commentary on Henri Alleg's infamous exposé, *La Question.* His activity during this decade was thus intense, often aided by stimulants. In 1958, suffering from liver trouble, headaches, and high blood pressure, he was very ill. Beauvoir attributed his blood pressure partly to the tension of "thinking against himself," that is, revising his positions, plus distress over events in Algeria and France (*FC,* 451).

The Last Decades

The twenty years between 1960 and Sartre's death from uremia in April 1980 are of less interest to the student of literature than the previous decades of his career, but are of prime importance to those interested in his political thought. His life continued much the same, until loss of sight in his left eye, formerly his good one, made it impossible for him to read and write. He also had high blood pressure, severe problems of circulation, which led to leg trouble, and cerebral and pulmonary difficulties in the 1970s (*C,* passim). In the 1960s he traveled extensively, often on invitation, including trips to Yugoslavia (whose Tito he admired), the USSR (almost every summer between 1962 and 1966), other European nations, Japan, Egypt, and Israel. He met with such heads of state as Tito, Khrushchev, Nasser, and Castro. In 1960 he and Beauvoir were invited to spend two months in Brazil and visit Cuba. He refused an invitation to lecture at Cornell University because he disapproved of the American war in Vietnam (*TCF,* 376). In 1965 he officially adopted a Jewish Algerian student, Arlette El Kaïm, whom he had met in 1956.[17] Before he was named winner of the Nobel Prize in 1964, he indicated he would refuse it, and publicly rejected it when it was voted anyway; his reasons included unwillingness to be "consecrated" or taken over by European humanism and the middle classes, that is, the desire to remain a radicalized figure (*WS,* 451–56; *SV,* 222; see also *C,* 324–25).

The list of causes Sartre espoused and the positions he took is too long to be reproduced. (See the chronology in *Œuvres romanesques* and *C,* passim.) His interests ranged from the wars in Algeria and Vietnam to politics in Poland, Hungary, and Cuba (where he saw the revolution being turned aside from its proper spirit), from the June 1967 Arab-Israeli war to Venezuelan resistance fighters and the Bretons and Occitans in France.[18] He took stands against apartheid and racism in general, on the Jewish problem in Russia, the Quebec separatist movement, the Basque question, and the May uprising of 1968, when he supported the students against the university and police (*TCF,* 472 ff.). In Brazil he was acclaimed more for his stand on Algeria than his writings, and in Paris rightist demonstrators displayed signs saying "Execute Jean-Paul Sartre." He signed the "Letter of 121," published in *Les Temps Modernes* in August 1960, and supported Francis Jeanson in his trial that year. Far from using his celebrity to achieve immunity, he insisted that he receive the same treatment as other critics of government policy, and explicitly asked to be included among those charged with signing the "121" protest.[19] Periodicals in which he and others attacked French policy and denounced torture were repeatedly confiscated, and his apartment was twice bombed. He presided in 1967 over the Russell War Crimes Tribunal in Sweden and then Denmark, which examined the conduct of the United States in Vietnam and judged it guilty of war crimes. In 1968 he condemned the Soviet intervention in Czechoslovakia, while reaffirming his support for socialism (*TCF*, 367), and began to draw close to French Maoists, editing and writing for several extreme left-wing publications, notably *La Cause du Peuple* (The People's cause) and *Libération,* and distributing copies in the streets (*TCF*, 478; *C,* 16). In 1974 he interviewed Baader of the Baader-Meinhof group and spoke in his favor, denouncing the conditions of his imprisonment. He also cooperated in organizing support of Vietnamese refugees fleeing after Communist takeover, protested against the invasion of Afghanistan, and favored boycotting the Moscow Olympics.[20]

In literature, Sartre published successive volumes of *Situations* (mostly political essays) and his massive study of Flaubert, *L'Idiot de la famille (The Family Idiot),* wrote film scripts, including one for John Huston's *Freud* (from which he later dissociated himself), did a study of the painter Tintoretto, who had long interested him, wrote prefaces, and adapted Euripides' *The Trojan Women.* His plays were revived in Paris and translated and produced in European capitals, where he attended several of the premieres; and some of his works were made into films and televised. When near-blindness made work impossible, he spent his time discussing politics with friends, supporting various causes, listening to the radio or to Beauvoir reading to him, discussing books with her, and especially listening to music, a pastime since his childhood, in which he was very well versed (*C,* passim; *S* X, 167–72). He gave several important interviews, including lengthy ones with John Gerassi, Pierre Victor (Benny Lévy), Michel Sicard, Michel Contat (*New York Review of Books,* 1975), Michel Rybalka and others, and Beauvoir (*C,* 165–559). During his last illness, he was cared for by friends, including Beauvoir, and his adoptive daughter.

Conclusion

Just as *L'Idiot de la famille* is an attempt to explain how "Gustave" became Flaubert as he is known today, *Les Mots* has been described as the author's effort to find out "how one can have become Jean-Paul Sartre."[21] It is true that, without being so narcissistic as Rousseau, Chateaubriand,

and Gide, Sartre was very much interested in himself and his evolving career, as an illustration, he said, of "the movement through which any writer, good or bad, gives himself objective form in his works" (*WS*, xi). It is in this light that the biographic facts outlined above should be understood, each an element of that total trajectory which Sartre recognized as true—even though he was only half in love with it—and which, "if it is true that one is nothing but what one has done," with the works themselves brings one as close as possible to seizing the Sartrean project, or what he came to call the lived or *vécu*. Although much literary criticism has recently subordinated the man to the work, Sartre reversed this procedure in his study of Flaubert, taking as his chief topic the writer's origins in his psychological makeup and relationship to his situation. Jeanson summarizes well the value of Sartre's biography by saying that it is not only the adventure of a man but also that of his thought (*SV*, 15). It is legitimate, then, to connect the works which will now be studied to their biographic context, which, very generally, is, as Sartre said, that of a "[classic] intellectual . . . what he is in the process of becoming" (*SH*, 104).

Chapter Two

Sartre's Philosophy through 1945: Phenomenology and Ontology

The Philosophic Background

Sartrean philosophy of the first period, from *L'Imagination* (1936) through *L'Existentialisme est un humanisme* (published in 1946), can be characterized as phenomenological existentialism. His method and attitude toward consciousness are close to Edmund Husserl's, with whose works, chiefly *Ideas,* he was well acquainted and to whom he acknowledged his debt. Yet his concern for the individual, for concrete experience and its meaning, and for the relationships between the self and the world puts him, despite differences, in the great existential tradition of Pascal, Kierkegaard, Nietzsche, and Heidegger.[1] Both these connections bear examination. But first it is necessary to sketch the Cartesian background, one of the greatest influences on Sartre's thought.

Cartesianism, part of the ordinary baggage of the educated Frenchman, can be taken as almost synonymous with French thought. It implies reliance on reason, especially a methodology which makes reason the chief means of any philosophic or scientific investigation. It takes as its starting principle the cogito, that is, the reality of thought and thus of the thinking subject, Descartes's position being that the thinker can doubt everything except the fact of his doubt, or thinking, and that thus his existence as a subject is posited. Thought itself is thus intuitive, i.e., it gives data which cannot be refuted (e.g., that the sum of the angles of a triangle equals 180°). Proceeding from this principle, Descartes asserted that the thinking subject could then arrive at other truths, by using his reason, following the deductive method—proceeding step by step from one intuitive truth to another, from the simpler to the more complex. Although the Cartesian method is particularly suitable for science, in conjunction with an empirical approach, it can also be applied to reasoning about thought itself, and all the experiences normally considered as inner or subjective; his rationalism does not exclude, thus, the authority of the reflecting subject, but rather is built on it.

Sartre is plainly within this rationalist tradition. While many of his conclusions are opposed to those of Descartes, and he is not just a deductive thinker, any more than he is an empiricist, the primacy of the reasoning subject, whose intuitions are indisputable, is shared by both philosophers, and later criticisms Sartre makes do not change the fact that he assumes the cogito throughout, even if he understands it somewhat differently from his predecessor.

Husserl's philosophic project was much like that of the French mathematician, to whom he is considerably indebted. He wanted to find a solid basis on which to ground knowledge, particularly the sciences, and a method for extending knowledge, not of the practical variety but knowledge about knowledge; his enterprise, which can be termed a search for a better conceptual framework, is thus close to both psychology and epistemology. As Descartes had discarded the scholastics' disputations, Husserl wished to discard a whole tradition of metaphysical speculation, especially certain Kantian ideas, and return to the most basic level of investigation, by the reflection of the mind on itself. To do so, he began with what appears, or the phenomenon—whence the name of his undertaking, dealing with the *logos* or rationale of phenomena. But what appears is not studied as itself, in the context of the world, but as it appears to consciousness; indeed, consciousness—its structure, its operations—is the true subject of Husserl's investigations, although he also wants to discover the principles governing various types of objects of consciousness. Consciousness perceives, imagines, judges, intuits, values, constructs, and thus gives meaning to the world. As in the Cartesian tradition, the intuitive data of consciousness, especially concerning essences, are taken to be indisputable. Intuition is "the presence of the thing," the confrontation of an object, perceptual or imaginary, not just reasoning about it, still less any mystical understanding.[2] This does not mean that consciousness immediately knows all, even about itself, or that reflection cannot make discoveries; on the contrary, it needs a method by which to achieve progressively greater revelation of what appears and how it appears; but the method is based on consciousness itself and its intuitive capacities. Husserl's philosophy is thus not empirical but relies rather on reflection. As for the context, the world in which and of which this consciousness is conscious, Husserl, rather than attempting to solve the old realist versus idealist dilemma concerning the reality or factuality of the world, sets it off, in "brackets," by a step which he calls the phenomenological reduction, abandoning the "thesis of the natural standpoint" (the daily supposition that we and the world exist) to say simply that pure consciousness and what appears to it will be studied. Whether or not appearance equals being is not essential to the reflections of consciousness either upon itself or upon that which appears, and, moreover, the data that consciousness gathers about itself, while revealing its own nature, cannot reveal the nature of what it is conscious of. (This is in opposition to an epistemological tradition that would reduce the knowledge of objects to knowledge concerning the activity of thought.) Husserl is thus led to an idealistic position—not that he affirms that the world does *not* exist, but that its existence is radically separate from our thought, which cannot know its laws.

When Raymond Aron, Sartre's predecessor at the Institut Français in Berlin, told him about Husserl, saying (it was in a bar) that one could, following Husserl's method, philosophize by talking about an apricot cocktail, he was greatly impressed; this was the kind of philosophy he had been looking for, dealing with the everyday, the concrete (*SH,* 26; *C,* 205). This may seem contradictory, since Husserl put the everyday world of cocktails and so forth into brackets. But it was justified insofar as Sartre was interested in how we are conscious of things, and Husserl's abstract investigations do take this consciousness for their subject. Sartre later expressed his disagreement with Husserl's idealistic reduction and affirmed rather that a proper phenomenological view of consciousness requires the presence of the existing world; furthermore, philosophy has nothing to gain by the world's being "reduced." In this sense, Sartre is a realist.

In the existentialist tradition, Heidegger is the chief influence. Sartre knew, of course, Pascal, Kierkegaard, and Nietzsche, but in spite of his insistence on the individual subject, the Christian perspectives of the first two, the oracular and visionary aspect of the third would not be attractive to him.[3] Heidegger stressed the search for the meaning of Being (usually capitalized). It is true that he was more interested in human reality than in the "brute existence" of things; Sartre, too, for that matter, though first of all he wished to study the situation of human reality in the world; ultimately both thinkers strove for a comprehensive view of the whole of existence. They are thus primarily devoted to ontology, the science of being. There is also similarity of outlook between them, a brooding, often anguished quality which one associates with Germanic writers, and yet the aspiration—which sets them apart from Kierkegaard—toward totality, the construction of a massive whole.

Other thinkers to whom Sartre was indebted on specific points include his philosophy professors and writers as diverse as Bergson and William James.[4] His reading was wide. Hegel and Marx, crucial influences later, were not consequential in the formation of his first philosophy, although known to him at the time. Generally speaking, he showed a remarkable capacity for synthesis, as well as analysis, combining in the same vision the rationalism of Descartes, the intuitive science which Husserl practiced, and Heidegger's quest for true Being, especially in the confrontation between matter and man. This synthesis found its finest expression in *L'Etre et le néant,* but initially Sartre approached the problem of man in the world through that of the functions of consciousness.

The Earliest Philosophic Works

Sartre's first four studies, *L'Imagination,* "La Transcendance de l'ego," *Esquisse d'une théorie des émotions,* and *L'Imaginaire,* reveal that his approach to philosophic problems, especially that of being, was through the study of the nature and operations of consciousness. His university thesis was the basis for the two studies on the imagination. He submitted a lengthy version to the publisher Alcan; of this, the first portion was published in 1936 as *L'Imagination;* the remainder later formed the basis for the lengthy study of 1940. Peter Caws suggested that Sartre was led to this topic by his literary interests, an interpretation since confirmed (*C,* 202–204); nevertheless, it was a crucial step in the development of a full-fledged ontology.[5]

The first essay is an historical critique of views on the mental image and the process of image-forming held by such writers as Descartes, Spinoza, Leibniz, Hume, Taine, Bergson, and Alain. They are all held to be erroneous to some degree, mainly because they make the image into an object which is *in* consciousness, as a copy, a false or degraded form of the real. Imagination thus becomes an inferior form of perception. This view leads to insoluble difficulties, especially the problem of how we distinguish between perception and imagination, since both would involve confrontation with things. Sartre asserts that no solution will be found without a radically different approach to the questions of consciousness and its relation to the world. He proposes Husserl's doctrine of intentionality, which remains fundamental throughout his philosophy.[6] It states very simply that all consciousness is consciousness of something.[7] Consciousness cannot be reduced to its activity; it always refers to an object, standing beyond it. This implies a radical separation between consciousness and that of which it is conscious, that is, between itself and the world, which is outside it, transcending it, and it excludes the world's being constituted by the *contents* of consciousness (as in Berkeley's idealism). This separation is the chief dualism in Sartre's early philosophy; in other respects he attempts to overcome traditional dualisms, especially the Cartesian ones between soul and body, reality and appearance, and duality within the self. He assigns to these two types of existence—consciousness and its object—the Hegelian terms *for-itself* and *in-itself*, which are crucial in *L'Etre et le néant*. In-itself is inert; for-itself is spontaneous, *ex nihilo*, without cause (thus also *by-itself*), simply bursting forth into the world. Consciousness includes self-awareness: "For consciousness, to exist is to be conscious of its existence" (2). This does not mean that it always deliberately or reflectively thinks about itself; there is no need for a reflective act for consciousness to be aware of being conscious, just as there is no need to think about acting in order to act.[8] (This feature is called its nonthetic or nonpositional quality.)[9] It can thus be termed unreflexive or prereflexive. However, it can turn on itself, becoming a reflexive or positional consciousness (125).

The object of which we are conscious in perception *exists;* the object reproduced in imagination similarly exists, but differently (unreally, he will say later); it cannot be explained as sense content in the mind. Consciousness apprehends directly an image as image, a perception as perception. The visible paper and the imagined paper have the same individual character and structure but exist on different planes; their essence is the same without their existence being so. In each case, consciousness is intending (going toward) its object, or correlate, which transcends consciousness (but not in a mystical sense), that is, stands apart from and goes beyond it. This view enabled Husserl, and Sartre after him, to eliminate most of the difficulties connected with the classical problem of the relation between material things called images (paintings, photographs) and mental images.

"La Transcendance de l'ego," one of the most interesting of Sartre's early works, was first published in *Recherches Philosophiques* in 1937 and later in volume form. It first considers briefly the Kantian view of the ego, then Husserl's contribution. Husserl claimed that a transcendental ego stands behind consciousness, as it were, as a formal principle of unification, interpreting its intended objects or identifying its "contents." Being pure subject instead of object, it is not part of the world, thus not subject to reduction.[10] This Sartre denies, trying to show that consciousness is not identical to a preconstituted "self" or "personality"; it is not a datum within consciousness or substantial. He asserts that the ego is derivative, that it exists, paradoxically, *for* consciousness rather than beyond or behind it, outside, a quasi-object. Consciousness can affirm its unity only reflexively. It does not need its contents interpreted for it, since it has no contents; all content is on the side of the object, even sense data, which we think of as being in our minds. Consciousness is impersonal spontaneity, an absolute, an activity transcending toward objects, always present to them.[11] "It is in the object that the unity of the consciousnesses is found" (38). In short, since consciousness is already aware of itself, it does not need a personality behind it to create this awareness. "It is consciousness . . . which makes possible the unity and the personality of my *I*" (40). But this does not mean that the "self" of which it is aware is a full-blown ego. Rather, it is "the spontaneous, transcendent unification of our states and our actions" (76).

Critics have pointed out various problems in this position, for instance, Sartre's contention that consciousness can be absolutely impersonal (37).[12] But the departure from Husserl was made in accordance with Husserl's own principle of intentionality, which, for Sartre, is not just one feature of consciousness; it *is* consciousness. The position is also consonant with Sartre's insistence on doing away with the notion of hidden selves, subject-object duality, and inner conflict, in favor of the unity and the transparency of consciousness—a concern he retained throughout his career. It may also have the effect of throwing a critical light on the phenomenological reduction (since, if there is no transcendental ego and consciousness is absolute transparency, without contents, a world is necessary for it to have any existence at all, and there is no pure or transcendental point from which to study consciousness, without reference to being).[13] Dispensing with Husserl's reduction would seem to have had fortunate consequences for the subsequent development of Sartrean thinking, which was to become occupied with concrete existence within the world, which Husserl always suspended. By his view of how the spontaneity of consciousness imprisons itself in a constituted ego in order to flee from itself, he even sketches out the concept of bad faith, elaborated later. Likewise, anguishing freedom, another key concept in *L'Etre et le néant*, is visible.

Esquisse d'une théorie des émotions, the "best introduction" to *L'Etre et le néant* (*WS*, 65), was extracted from an unfinished longer manuscript. Sartre proposes to use the phenomenological method of study, which differs from a psychological approach, to arrive at an understanding of the essential *structure* of emotion, by studying consciousness and its objects. Emotion must be considered as significant, rather than merely existing; studied as an organized form of consciousness, it helps answer the question, "What must consciousness be like for emotion to be possible?" First Sartre treats the classical theories, chiefly those of William James and Pierre Janet. He then examines the psychoanalytic explanations, which assign to the unconscious the role of organization and meaning of the emotion, which expresses itself symbolically. This makes of consciousness a secondary and passive phenomenon—a view contradicted by his notion of the cogito, according to which consciousness has absolute proximity to itself, is never anything but what it appears to be, and is at once the signification and the thing signified. Sartre thus argues against the unconscious. He does not deny symbolization but insists that there is an immanent bond of comprehension between the symbol and the symbolizing.

Sartre notes the unreflexive nature of emotion: fear is not consciousness of being afraid, it is consciousness of the world, or more precisely, an awareness of the world, a certain way of apprehending it. Normally, the world is seen as a complex of instruments organized so that one can produce a determined effect by using this instrumentality. But at times of great difficulty or resistance, the world is seen as noninstrumental, non-determined. In this case one acts not through a series of causes and effects but immediately and, as it were, through magic. Emotion, Sartre says, is a magical transformation through our body of the world, or of our relation to it, so that it appears to change its qualities. For instance, freezing in fear is a way of denying the world, when one lacks power to meet the danger by normal instrumental methods. Emotion is, in short, a mode of existence of consciousness. It is not something one *has;* it is a conscious, chosen way of being aware of the world.

Whereas its short predecessor was mainly a historical critique, *L'Imaginaire* consists of a fully developed phenomenology of the image, based in part on experiments by such psychologists as Binet and Sartre's friend Daniel Lagache. Many key Sartrean concepts are introduced or elaborated here. Sartre begins by stating his method—reflection of consciousness on itself—and affirming that the data of the image are absolutely certain, that the image is a type of consciousness *sui generis.* While perception is perspectival and "overflows" consciousness (one *must* adopt a point of view, yet an object can always be observed from another point of view), the image contains nothing more than consciousness has put there and includes the knowledge of itself. It is positional, i.e., it posits its object, but in its own way; one is conscious of an object, not of an *image* of an object. Perception posits its object as existence; conception (which can use the image unreflectively) as a positive essence; imagination as a nothingness. The image is a negation because it posits its object either as nonexistent (a centaur) or absent (not here) or existing elsewhere (and thus not here), or as neutral, i.e., in suspending belief. Whether a purely mental image or a graphic one such as a painting, the image "stands for" its object as its analogon.

The second part of the treatise suggests the nature of the analogon in the mental image, in such classic cases as love and desire. Sartre also discusses the relationship of words to images, which interests Roquentin in *La Nausée*. In part three he explores the relationship of the image to symbols, thought, and perception. Images are not supports or illustrations for thoughts; they *are* a type of thought, which "realizes" qualities in a pictured object instead merely of affirming them, that is, where thought appears as object. They do not stand for the unknown, otherwise incomprehensible, but rather often express comprehension. The image is not the product of an association because it cannot be caused from the outside; like other modes of consciousness, it is self-constituted according to its own intentionality. Images and perceptions are the two great irreducible attitudes of consciousness, neither one being combined with the other (since one cannot imagine what he perceives, nor perceive the imagined). The fourth part treats dreams, hallucinations, and other pathological occurrences of imagination, emphasizing again that the contents of imagination are known in advance to the knower and thus excluding the hypothesis of the unconscious. Sartre's conclusions are that consciousness can imagine because it can *unrealize,* posit a thesis of unreality, that is, negate. It can do this because it is able to grasp the world in its synthetic totality and is not itself in-the-middle-of-the-world, as its objects are, but separate. That is, consciousness is free, even if it depends on the world to have something to negate; it is absolutely given. Imagination is both evidence and exercise of freedom. But it must be exercised from a certain point of view; Sartre calls this a situation, "the different immediate ways of apprehending the real as a world."[14]

L'Etre et le néant

The *magnum opus* of Sartre's first period, *L'Etre et le néant* (1943), which attracted attention slowly, furnishes the most commonly known elements of his thought. It is also a key companion piece to his literary works. For these reasons, as well as its intrinsic interest, it deserves close attention, despite obscurities, excessively long technical arguments, and other flaws.[15] Sartre's purpose is to create an ontology by using the phenomenological approach borrowed from Husserl and modified. He is led particularly to examine man, that being who interrogates being, who asks what it means to be (Heidegger's *Dasein*), for it is clear that the position of the questioner of being who himself *is* is a privileged one. The distinction between man and what he questions, or for-itself and in-itself, is fundamental throughout.[16] (Sartre does call for-itself a type of being, although it will later be revealed as nothingness.) He is more interested in human reality than in the being of the world, which he rather neglects, except for its contrasts to consciousness. The scientific approach to how the world is revealed does not interest him, and his views are inadequate for certain problems posed by the existence of the physical universe, though he does have some remarkable things to say about embodiment. In addition, he leaves aside questions he calls metaphysical, that is, relating to origins and reasons for existence. His view is that metaphysical questioning reveals only contingency (lack of necessity). Ontologically speaking, beginnings are simply the "pure event" (*BN,* 89), when being denies and negates itself, thus becoming something separate from being, called consciousness. This point is neither historical, religious, nor scientific; it is simply the original bursting forth of consciousness. However, Sartre *is* led, because of his focus on human reality, to treat some classic problems in philosophy, such as time. He also focuses on relationships with oneself and others; these are among his most provocative pages. In addition, he moves toward, but does not treat in detail, principles of ethics.

Sartre's introductory definition of the phenomenon as what appears (*BN,* xlvi) eliminates the classic being versus appearance dualism; he needs, however, to investigate the "being" of this appearing if he wants to treat standard ontological problems. Since appearances logically "lay claim to a being which is no longer itself appearance" (*BN,* lvii)—that is, since what appears calls for something else to which to appear—he immediately moves to consciousness, or for-itself. He recalls Husserl's principle of intentionality, which means that the cogito refers immediately to something which is not itself, and the absolute separation between consciousness and its object, which goes beyond it. "Consciousness is born *supported by* a being which is not itself. This is what we call the ontological proof" (*BN,* lxi; Sartre's emphasis). Consciousness is not, however, equivalent to knowledge. It is unreflexive or prereflexive, nonpositional, that is, unreflecting on but aware of itself. Only when it becomes reflexive, turning on itself, is it a quasi-knowledge. Consciousness exists and is determined only *by*-itself (which does not mean it creates itself in a causal relationship); it is not dependent upon chance but rather is an absolute. It is also a unity; there can be no real division in consciousness, although it can reflect on itself.

Sartre rejects all creationist theories of the origin of being in-itself. Yet it is not its own cause either; it simply is itself. Being precedes non-being and thus has primacy with respect to consciousness: consciousness comes to annihilate being, not the reverse. Being has no inside, no secret, no becoming; it is massive; it is passive. It has no relationship of any kind, not even one of otherness, with what is not itself. It is pure positiveness. No part of the in-itself can reveal itself; this is up to consciousness.

Part I is an investigation of negativity and nothingness, which, as *L'Imaginaire* indicated, is associated with what is not in-itself, or consciousness. Man, Sartre notes, is a being who questions, and all questioning carries within it the possibility of a negative answer, just as all negating and even affirming are negative positions. (If I say, "This is my friend," I am saying also, "This is not my enemy," "This is not a table," etc.) But is linguistic negation at the *source* of nothingness, or does it *spring from* nothingness? Or is it merely a phenomenon of language? Sartre says that it springs from nothingness, which is at the heart of human reality; it is "the putting into question of being by being" (*BN,* 79), a "hole" in the heart of being, an appeal to being. He thus argues against Hegel's understanding of negation and adopts a viewpoint closer to Heidegger's. Nothingness, of course, cannot be the same as being and must somehow be given from the outside. Man is the being by whom nothingness comes into the world. What is man like for this to be possible? Free, answers Sartre, free to secrete a nothingness which isolates him. And this nothingness is what separates consciousness from its own past, as well as from its future; human essence is always having-been, and we constitute human nature behind us, rather than being determined by it. The for-itself makes itself temporally; one cannot say that it *is.* Human reality is *"the being which is always beyond its being-there"* (*BN,* 549; Sartre's emphasis).

For both Sartre and Heidegger, man becomes aware of this nothingness in anguish, felt particularly with respect to value: no value has any foundation other than in human liberty, and nothing justifies the choice of one value over another. (Sartre thus adumbrates a connection between ontology and ethics.) "In anguish I apprehend myself at once as totally free and as not being able to derive the meaning of the world except as coming through myself" (*BN,* 40). To anguish, flight is the immediate response, especially in the form of a deterministic view—seeing oneself like a thing, from the outside. But flight is unsuccessful, because in order to flee we must be aware of the anguish we are fleeing (just as thinking I do not want to think of something is still thinking of it): the unity of consciousness precludes total escape. "Flight from anguish is only a mode of becoming conscious of anguish" (*BN*, 43). The negating power which denies anguish, yet denies itself so that I may *affirm* anguish to flee it, is bad faith.

Sartre goes to pains to distinguish the important concept of bad faith from ordinary lying, in which one is conscious of the truth he conceals, and to indicate that it is not unconscious either. The explanation by the unconscious destroys psychic unity and creates still further problems, since, in order for Freudian censure to operate, the mind must be conscious of what it hides in the unconscious, in which case it is in bad faith—an argument which supposes what it tries to explain. Bad faith is neither "cynical lie, nor knowing preparation for deceitful concepts. . . . The first act of bad faith is to flee what it cannot flee, to flee what it is" (*BN*, 70). It is a mode of being, which implies both division and unity; one masks the truth to oneself, while knowing it is the truth. In passing Sartre analyzes both belief and sincerity, key concepts in modern criticism. To believe is, paradoxically, not to believe—to be at a distance from the affirmed belief. Similarly, in sincerity a man constitutes himself to be what he is not; he tries to make himself coincide with his being.

In the second main part of the treatise, concerned with the for-itself, Sartre first contrasts it with in-itself.[17] The latter coincides with itself; the former is fissure and distance. It is also presence to itself; but this does not mean a full, noble self-consciousness, in the humanist tradition, but rather separation. One cannot even say that the for-itself *is*. At most it *is been*—at a distance. "The for-itself is the being which determines itself to exist inasmuch as it cannot coincide with itself." It is "the original project of its own nothingness" (*BN*, 78–79). In-itself is contingent, unforeseen, a matter of chance, and thus without foundation, whereas consciousness, Sartre repeats, is by-itself, its own possibility; it is perpetually tearing itself away by its negating activity (one would say it creates, except that creation implies a created object). However, the for-itself is "haunted by" contingency. Sartre's elaborate technical arguments to demonstrate this are less effective than his appeal to common experience: why is our consciousness embodied, why is a particular presence in the world granted to us, why are we born in such-and-such circumstances? The recognition of this contingency, which Heidegger said led to authenticity and culpability, for Sartre means feeling gratuitous, unjustified, superfluous. To this complex of contingency—the fact that we cannot found our presence—he gives the name facticity.

He next analyzes the notions of desire, lack, and possibility, which are structures of the for-itself, which introduces them into the world, and indeed thus brings about that there *is* a world, instead of just brute matter. Once one has associated for-itself with fissure and noncoincidence with itself, it is easy to comprehend lack, which is a failure of being. It is *we* who perceive things in terms of lack according to our projects and desires; we see lacks because we are ourselves lack. Similarly, desire is lack of being, and man is fundamentally *desire to be*. More precisely, the for-itself, while keeping its freedom, translucidity of consciousness and self-foundation, aspires to be, like the in-itself. Such a being, if conceivable, would be God; unfortunately, Sartre says, it is contradictory, and God does not exist. "Man fundamentally is the desire to be God" (*BN,* 566).[18] By desire, we constitute things as desirable and thus erect values. Possibility is like lack; it is our own mode of being, what the for-itself lacks to be itself, and we perceive things in its terms; a cloud is a possibility of rain not because of the laws of nature but because man "projects" onto clouds his own potentiality. Indeed, the whole world is ours as a correlative of our nothingness; it is our necessary obstacle, haunted by our possibilities.

Possibility is connected with time. The nothingness which separates human reality from itself is the source of temporality, which arises because we are not identical, always at a distance from ourselves, so that time is not something into which we are plunged but is an aspect of the cogito, our way of being conscious of ourselves. Past, present, and future are not an infinite series of nows added together but structured moments of an original synthesis. Sartre argues against the views on time of Descartes, Kant, and Bergson, among others. His view is that our past is the "ever growing totality of the in-itself which we are" (*BN,* 115). We are not this in the mode of identity (since we are not anything in that mode) but in the mode of what-we-have-to-be, or the past tense. In the past all possibility is extinguished; yet we are totally responsible for it. A past is not something one *has;* it is the "ontological structure which obliges me to be what I am *from behind*" (*BN,* 118; Sartre's emphasis). The present is obviously presence-to: to the in-itself; for-itself is the being by whom such presence comes into the world. Likewise, the future arrives through for-itself; it is our flight toward the in-itself we want to be. The nature of man is, in Valéry's phrase, "an always future hollow." One can never catch up with in-itself; the future simply becomes the past, one's facticity. "We run toward ourselves, and we are—due to this very fact—the being which cannot be reunited with itself" (*BN*, 202). Sartre's famous utterance, "To be free is to be condemned to be free" (*BN*, 129), means that man can escape neither into the future nor the past; he will never coincide with solid, massive being, except in death, in which his total life is past and thus he is entirely facticity and in-itself.

The term *transcendence* describes the original relation between human reality and the world. One of its aspects is knowledge, since in knowing we obviously go beyond ourselves to something else. All knowledge is intuitive, that is, presence of consciousness to the thing. This presence consists not in a "relationship" but in pure identity denied. One mode of knowledge is space; another is movement. These are not properties of in-itself, but aspects of negation, which do not modify being. Other such aspects are quality, quantity, potentiality, functionality, and beauty. Utensils, for instance, are "the exact correlative of my possibilities," the projected image of me (*BN*, 200).

Part III deals with what is called being-for-others and consciousness in its relationship with other consciousnesses, and, since they can be its mediators, with itself in a body. Sartre first states the classic problem: how can one be sure of the existence of others? After examining various erroneous views, particularly the thesis of solipsism (complete enclosure within the self), he proposes characteristic arguments to show that we do not deduce the existence of others but rather that others reveal to us our own existence; they are our mediators. This argument depends considerably on an appeal to common experiences, especially those of shame, pride, and fear, which disclose us to ourselves as an object for another. It is by being thus objectified that we discover the indubitable existence of others. The appearance of another in my world first decentralizes it, then by constituting itself as subject objectifies me. "For me the other is first the being for whom I am an object . . . *through whom* I gain my objectness" (*BN*, 270; Sartre's emphasis). No Husserlian reduction can change this. I depend on others *in my being* (and Hegel saw this, in his master-slave analysis); my transcendent relationship with them constitutes my being proper; and it is their existence which makes the cogito possible. A privileged form of this objectification by others is their gaze. My permanent possibility of being seen by someone, who constitutes *himself* as subject whereas *I* had first seen *him* as object, is my original relationship to others, who are defined as those who look at me. By being objectified, I become the one whom the other knows. I am without defense before this freedom which is not mine. Not that I can truly coincide with myself; Sartre reaffirms this as impossible. But for the other, I am fixed, like an object. "My original fall is the existence of the other" (*BN,* 263). Sartre calls this threatening relationship alienation, a term to which he later gives a Marxist meaning.

The next section, on embodiment, is concerned with two problems especially: the relationship of the body to consciousness and the relationship between bodies, especially our being-for-others. One senses here, as in other Sartrean works, that the author was not at ease with his own body; there is none of the sense of physical pleasure and the delights of sensation and activity found, for instance, in some of the lyrical writings of Gide and Camus.[19] The body is defined as the "*contingent form which is assumed by the necessity of my contingency*" (*BN,* 309; Sartre's emphasis). It is contingent that we be in such-and-such a body, but we must be in *some* body. Our body is thus our presence, our engagement in the world. It is not an addition to us, as the body is to the soul in traditional dualism. It is our orientation toward the world, in which we must always adopt a point of view on everything except the body itself; it *is* our point of view, on which we can take no point of view. Whereas we utilize other objects, we *exist* our body, in Sartre's term. The revelation of our body is not primary, however; it comes to us secondarily, through the complex of other objects (utensils), to which we relate through it, and, as Sartre shows in a discussion of pain, we normally go beyond it, just as in language we go beyond sign toward meaning. The "taste" of our prereflexive awareness of the body is called nausea; it is our original reaction, not a particular disgust inspired by an outside object but simply the reaction to being flesh. The body of the other can give this reaction to us, when it is seen as pure contingency or, more basically, by pointing out to us our corporality; another's body is radically different from mine in that I *can* take a point of view on it, but it also indicates my own. Moreover, by his subjectivity (his look) the other can take perspectives on my body that I cannot and can objectify me; he thus transcends me, and my body is the awareness of being transcended. This explains reactions of timidity—blushing—and the truism that others see us as we really are (*BN,* 354).

Sartre's chapter on concrete relations with others, such as love and hatred, important literary themes, confirms many of the implications of his fiction and theater and gives them a foundation, in terms chiefly of a subject-object dualism, though later in his career he denied validity to such dualism. The notion of facticity is essential—not that our body causes our relations with others, but that it constitutes our situation and limits with respect to them. Reactions to others are of two kinds, both of which involve the freedom of the other: either love, language, and masochism on the one hand, or indifference, desire, hatred, and sadism on the other. In all cases, the original meaning of human relationships is conflict, which can be overcome only fleetingly, so that all human relationships are doomed to failure. All of these modes except indifference are basically sexual. Sexuality and desire in general express an original effort of for-itself to recuperate its being alienated by others. In love, one wants to possess or appropriate the other's freedom, given up *freely*, specifically by being loved in return (which creates an endless reflexive relationship: to love is to want to be loved). But freely to give up one's freedom means that it is not truly abandoned, since the abandon itself is founded in freedom. The love project is thus self-defeating. The lover dreams of identifying the love object with himself, while nevertheless preserving its individuality—a hopeless effort. Language is not something added to our relationships with others but rather *is* originally our being-for-others, directed toward the freedom of others, who must recognize it and give it its meaning. Masochism is the stance adopted when one despairs of founding his subjectivity in the other and instead desires to make himself an object, letting being-for-others cover the basic for-itself project; one is then wholly alienated. This leads to culpability; it is a failure, since consciousness of one's subjectivity or transcendence remains.

Indifference or "blindness" is a type of bad faith; it denies the freedom of the other. Like all bad faith, it fails because by denying the true otherness of those around him, the subject is thrown back on his own liberty, his pure, anguishing for-itself. Sexual desire is similar in that it tries to seize the subjectivity of the other through his objectness. Far from believing that sexual instinct is primary, Sartre asserts that it is the secondary expression of our basic being-for-others; though fundamental to all human relationships and all-pervasive, as Freud had suggested in an entirely different approach, sexuality is just the instrumentation of the basic structure for others.[20] Desire is the attempt to appropriate another consciousness as incarnate, and thus to bring it into servitude. Sadism is a particular form of the desire to enslave the other in his facticity, while preserving one's own freedom. The sadist tries to "englue" the other in his flesh, thus imprisoning and appropriating his freedom. One means is to reduce the other's body to pure obscenity—flesh deprived of function, meaning, and grace. But sadism too is a failure, for, as in love, giving up oneself, even under torture, is still a free act, so that the other's freedom thus reasserts itself; this is visible in the tortured person's look.

All attempts to alienate one's own freedom or possess that of others are thus doomed to failure because of the basic structure of being-for-others, founded on the totally free for-itself. Even altruism and tolerance are impositions on others, no matter how lofty our principles: in treating another tolerantly, I force him to react to tolerance; in freeing someone, I require him to be free. All human relationships are thus guilty. Even hatred or the other's death cannot change this: his death constitutes me as an object for him forever (as he judged me), and hatred merely recognizes the claim of the other on me. To this gloomy picture no relief is offered, except by a footnote suggesting that an "ethics of salvation" would be possible after a "radical conversion"—a topic not further elaborated, but which, in a sense, all Sartre's career from the mid-1950s on is an effort to illustrate (*BN,* 412).

Can any human community—what Heidegger calls *Mitsein* or being-with—be built in the structure of being-for-others? Sartre's answer in 1943 is no. Psychological and social bonds can be created, leading to an apparent *we,* by the presence of a third party; but this is not a basic structure of our being. While others' gaze or judgment can create an *us* relationship (objects of a third)—as the solidarity of the working class is created by its objectivity for the bourgeoisie—there is no such thing as a genuine *we* as subject, and humanity as a whole has no community, since there is no separate third—God—to see us thus.

Implications of this ontology and familiar philosophic problems such as freedom and death are raised in the final part of *L'Etre et le néant.* Freedom has usually been confused with power. But ontological freedom is not omnipotence or power to obtain an end but freedom to choose that end— "by oneself to determine oneself to wish" (*BN,* 483)—to organize the world toward that end. It is total, limited only by itself (my necessity to be free, and the freedom of others). It is the first condition of action and is itself act: we do not first perceive ourselves as free and then decide to act, but rather action is the realization of our freedom. Sartre uses the term *project* or *pro-ject* to show that time itself is an aspect of freedom: we project ourselves forward, acting toward a future end. So that freedom does not mean pure caprice, senseless wavering, or unpredictability; on the contrary, since we act in view of something, our choices are thereby molded and often foreseeable. Yet they are not determined; it is not a question of fixed character. A concept important in his later biographical studies appears here, that of original choice or fundamental project, which is not a Freudian trauma or any other determining factor, but rather a basic choice of oneself as a certain type of being, and subsequent action which is consistent with this choice. It is always revocable; there are conversions, changes of character, inexplicable and sudden decisions, which mean a denial of the earlier project. But as long as the project is adhered to—and this is done freely—action is directed toward its realization, and thus represents the living out of liberty. Will and the passions, which in both Cartesian and popular thought are taken to be at odds in human character, struggling for dominance, are neither one determining but rather are both aspects of choice; they are intentional, ways of constituting freedom, or self-determination.

Apparent restrictions and objections to this view of freedom include facticity; but, far from preventing freedom, facticity actually allows it, since choice and action would be meaningless in a world without in-itself. Obstacles are what makes choice possible; omnipotence would destroy the very meaning of freedom. No matter what one's facticity, one can always project (not merely wish for) a certain future, even in prison (by the project to escape, to create a community with fellow-prisoners, etc.). (This view of freedom Sartre was later to see as naive.) Related to facticity is the concept of situation, that is, our position in the world defined by its obstacles or "coefficient of adversity" (resistance or suitability for us), in relation to a freely chosen end. Rather than being a limit to it, situation is that in which we exercise our freedom.

Various aspects of facticity and situation bear examination. Our place (birth, race, etc.) and what surrounds us seem to limit us, as do others and the past. But these are not true limitations. Though the past as fact cannot be changed, it does not exist anyway; what exists is the interpretation, the value I choose to give to the past (my own, history). Others' freedom, while apparently determining (since I must assume my being-for-others), is efficacious only so long as I recognize it and accept their judgments. Sartre gives the example of the Jew, who must see himself on the basis of others' classification of him as Jewish but is free to assume or reject this, be a Zionist, be ashamed, etc. Even death is not a limit to freedom, in the proper sense. Rather, it is beyond freedom. Arguing against Heidegger's view that death is the supreme human possibility, Sartre shows that it is an extinction of possibilities, whether it is suicide, death by accident, death in old age; it is absurd, and discussing it in relationship to freedom is meaningless, since it does not belong to the structure of the for-itself.

The conclusion to these remarks is the well-known, if disquieting, principle that man is responsible not only for himself but for the world. By responsible Sartre means conscious "of being the uncontestable author of an event or of an object" (BN, 553). Human reality is without excuse, and everyone is responsible for such apparently impersonal events as war (as he shows in a later novel), since we are the ones who make the world come into being by our freedom, and we are always free to react to events by approving or condemning. We are not responsible only for having been born; in that sense only we are "abandoned" or forsaken.

Existential psychoanalysis, a major concern here, does have some points in common with Freudian theory, but Sartre is careful to stress the differences. It is based on the theses of the unity of consciousness and the totality and basic project which each intention of the for-itself expresses. All acts are significant or "symbolic"; all attitudes are choices; and all choices, no matter what their form, are basically desire to *be*. Existential psychoanalysis proposes to discover the subject's original project, which can be expressed by any attitude, including the freely chosen ones called complexes.

Sartre is next concerned to show how having and doing are reducible to being: all doing is effort to have (whether it is really making something or simply performing), and having is a way of expressing desired self-identity through the possessed object, the "strong term" of the equation owner=owned. The relationship between property and oneself and the identity of money, power, and the self are ready illustrations. Even art and knowledge are a form of possession, thus of being. The ludic impulse is likewise reducible: playing is a manifestation of doing, thus of being. Sartre analyzes skiing as play, especially as an attempt to possess the snowy field by sliding over a substance which ordinarily will not hold a person and which is reducible to water. He concludes that "I search behind the phenomenon to possess the being of the phenomenon. . . . To possess is to wish to possess the world across a particular object" (*BN*, 597).

A final discussion treats quality as revealing of being. Existential psychoanalysis is concerned with establishing the way in which each thing is an objective symbol of being and its relationship to for-itself. The chief example is the important category of the viscous, or slimy, which, says Sartre, we react to and interpret as children without being taught to do so. Why is such a quality, which should be neutral, significant? Because it offers a horrible image to consciousness. Water attracts: it offers the picture of transparency, freedom, and fluidity with which consciousness identifies.[21] Solid objects are reassuring because they have the full, heavy being to which consciousness aspires. The viscous is like a trap: it would imprison consciousness in its sticky thingness while refusing to flow; yet it is not solid. It is a disgusting softness. "The horror of the slimy is the horrible fear that time might become slimy, that facticity might progress continually and insensibly and absorb the for-itself which *exists it*" (*BN*, 611; Sartre's emphasis). It is thus a symbol of an antivalue—what man does not want.

Sartre concludes by deciding that man wishes to avoid the contingency of the world and transform himself into a for-itself-in-itself, which would be its own foundation; this is his passion. Such an *ens causa sui,* or God, is impossible, and man is a "useless passion." He does recognize that, even if this ontological analysis is sound, problems remain, for instance, the metaphysical one, and the apparent dualism at the heart of his system. But the for-itself and the in-itself are not juxtaposed; they are in an internal synthesis, and one without the other is only an abstraction, like form without color, so that together they compose a totality, which is being. This is, however, a detotalized totality, a synthesis which is never completed, simply projected. The final problem Sartre recognizes is that of ethics, principles for which can be derived from his ontology. They would include the total equivalence of all action—since all aims at bringing about being for human reality, and all is doomed to failure—but the relative superiority of what is most lucid, based on the recognition that man is the being by whom all values come about and that none is sacred.

As an ontological exposition, *L'Etre et le néant* is both fascinating and annoying. At times the reader feels that Sartre is playing with words, pushing paradox to the limit, and drawing from language more than it can legitimately render. Yet his analyses and commentaries on human relationships, to take just one example, provoke the uneasiness which comes from recognition of true, if unpleasant, insights. In later writings he is concerned to go beyond the subjectivism of his ontology to give increased value to situations and groups.

L'Existentialisme est un humanisme

In this famous lecture of 1945, Sartre furnished a practical guide on what to take from *L'Etre et le néant.* It has been criticized for its lack of rigor (and he himself noted its shortcomings), but that flaw helped make it the popular statement it has become. The ethical element, which is very important and goes beyond the foundation set in the earlier work, does not have sufficient grounding. Sartre was aware of the need for a rigorous existentialist ethics and worked on it for some years (*SH,* 78, 81); Beauvoir's *Pour une morale de l'ambiguïté (The Ethics of Ambiguity)* was an attempt to remedy its lack.

The lecture was directed to postwar Frenchmen looking for principles of conduct in a society in upheaval; it was also intended to counter criticism, especially from Catholics and Marxists (neither seemed much swayed by it). In a direct and nontechnical manner, Sartre first sketches the various criticisms of existentialism, chiefly that it is a somber, pessimistic doctrine, and then proceeds to show that it is really optimistic, because it provides man with choice. Man is that being whose existence precedes its essence—unlike created objects, always made for a particular function. He is nothing and can be only what he makes himself; he is alone, without God; there is no human nature, and life has no given meaning. This implies responsibility, not only for oneself but for all, since each act proposes an image of man as we think he should be. This sense of responsibility leads to anguish, illustrated by the Kierkegaardian example of Abraham. Anguish is related to action, as a sign of choice.

According to what principles is one to act? Sartre gives an example which has become famous: a young man during the Occupation trying to decide whether to stay home and take care of his unhappy mother or leave to fight with the Free French based in England. To each particular problem, he says, there must be an individual solution, which is not found by following ready-set values but which rather creates these values: it is not *because* I believe in love that I remain with someone, but, remaining with him, I call that act love. So-called existentialist despair is simply the attitude that one must count upon oneself. Sartre notes that this disturbs people because it means they cannot be judged on what might have been and are responsible for their failures and character flaws. As for the accusation of subjectivism, he shows how the cogito is necessary for any truth to be possible at all, but how it also reveals others to us as well as ourselves. There is, moreover, a shared human condition, if not a human nature. One is always in a situation.

Having quoted Dostoyevsky's "If God does not exist, everything is permitted," Sartre must show that this does not mean capricious behavior or the Gidean gratuitous act; total responsibility leads to the obligation to create morality (as one creates a work of art). But it *does* mean that a project lucidly and sincerely chosen is valid in itself, not generally subject to judgment from others. Bad faith is different: it is blamable, since it denies what is true (freedom). Moreover—and here Sartre adumbrates important future developments—since liberty is fundamental, man is obliged to take it as its own aim, to make it the foundation of all values, and to seek it everywhere on the concrete plane. Where practical freedom is limited, as by political and social barriers, he must enhance it, to be consistent with ontological freedom. This is the clearest ethical statement in Sartrean philosophy through 1945.

Two important categories arise in this connection: cowards, those who hide from themselves their fundamental freedom; and *salauds* (usually translated as "bastards"), those who claim their existence is necessary. Humanism in the ordinary meaning of the word is unacceptable; it is a cult rendered to the fixed idea of what man is, and it leads to Fascism. By Sartrean humanism is meant the conviction that man is responsible for man, and that he projects himself out into the world. It is, in short, the attempt to draw from a coherent atheism its logical conclusions.

Chapter Three

The Early Fiction

La Nausée

Sartre's first novel is also his finest from a literary standpoint and the richest philosophically. Though begun when he was not yet thirty, it is in no sense an apprentice work.[1] Perhaps this is because it went through several versions. Like numerous other first novels, its aim is to represent life as a whole. But whereas many novice writers attempt to portray abstractly great feelings and ideas, Sartre's text is rooted in concrete experience and derives much of its strength from its controlled closeness to the quotidian and its physical correlatives for emotional and intellectual life. It is an exploration of the basic relationships between consciousness and the world. It is thus an excellent introduction to Sartrean ontology, even though the latter had not been entirely worked out by the mid-1930s.

Finished in 1936, it was accepted for publication the next year, following a slight misunderstanding, and appeared in 1938. Gaston Gallimard, the publisher, persuaded Sartre to change the title "Melancholia" (after Dürer's engraving) to *La Nausée*—a fortunate change, as Beauvoir later realized (*PL,* 239).[2] It is in the form of a diary, found, according to "notes from the editor," among the papers of Antoine Roquentin.[3] Since the latter is an historian working on a biography of a late eighteenth-century figure, this well-worn fictional convention borrowed from the same period is appropriate. It allows Sartre not to say what happened to the hero; the likelihood is that he is dead, or crazy, and thus the projects recorded in his diary receive from the beginning an ironic qualification.

Sometimes seen as nearly plotless, *La Nausée* does have a structure, well done if simple, comparable to that of quest and adventure stories; and the denouement brings about discoveries and an appropriate resolution. What makes it different from much other fiction is that the events are chiefly mental, set in motion by very ordinary incidents, and the search is an

39

epistemological one. Roquentin begins his diary in an attempt to find out something. Discovery by verbalization is a frequent motif in *L'Etre et le néant* and other modern works; Butor's *L'Emploi du temps (Passing Time)* comes to mind. Since *La Nausée* is not restrospective, one does not have the viewpoint that a narrator wiser than the reader can provide. Roquentin's quest takes place day to day in a banal setting, and involves mainly his consciousness of himself through his relationship with others and objects. Making the trivial revealing is one of Sartre's strengths.

Except for a brief episode in Paris, the action takes place in Bouville (Mudville), modeled on Le Havre, a bastion of the hated bourgeoisie. The characters are few: Roquentin, waitresses and café proprietors, a fellow patron of the library called the Autodidact (Self-Taught Man), Anny, the hero's former mistress, and a few others. The very antiheroic hero is nearly solitary, almost without for-others, reduced to his own consciousness, his own body, and objects. "I have no friends. Is that why my flesh is so naked?"[4] Since he is not employed, he is practically functionless. His case is thus extreme, suitable for study. Even his language is a little rusty; since he rarely tells anything to anyone, his thought often remains at a preverbal stage. His narrative begins, in a traditional way, with something new. He feels that things have changed, and he wants to determine exactly how by writing up the facts of his existence, the better to classify and analyze them. His is a very French enterprise, based on the desire to see clearly. He discovers that what has changed is not things themselves but the relationship between him and them (for-itself and in-itself). He senses this in the new way that objects now have of getting themselves picked up—a fork, a pipe. At the beach, he was unable to throw a pebble into the sea. He cannot pick up a paper in the street, although usually he likes discarded papers, both dry and muddy. He is afraid, and tentatively concludes that he is no longer free. He is particularly sensitive to certain qualities—the viscous, the hard, the ambivalent. His "nausea in the hands" (11) with respect to things extends to his own facticity. He devotes the rest of his diary to exploring the change in his perceptions and discovering its consequences for himself.

His ruminations turn around several topics. One of the first is his own body. Like Sartre as a child (*W,* 67), he stares at himself and grimaces in the mirror, trying to catch a meaning, an essence, to grasp himself as both object and subject. But a mirror image, as Sartre shows in *L'Etre et le néant,* is not a perspective on ourselves; it is seeing ourselves either as another or as pure carnality, reduced to the level of protoplasm, which swallows the meaning only a consciousness can give to it. In either case, his flesh is alienated from him. It appears bestial, and he feels it is full of nothingness. As his hand loses its function and meaning, ordinarily felt from the inside, he compares it to a crab. He finally pierces it with a penknife—thus recognizing its otherness and yet attempting to turn its inertness into possibility. But all that happens is the dripping out of a little blood—more in-itself. Consciousness can neither lose itself completely in the exterior world and its own facticity nor dominate it completely; whence the ambivalent feeling which is translated by nausea. This is why he is bothered by things that seem to go only halfway, notably Adolphe's suspenders, of an uncertain hue between purple and blue. They mirror his own embodiment; their brute existence showing through points to what he will later realize, that all qualities such as color are abstractions and do not exist; they merely cover over existence. To flee from existence, Roquentin would like to become pure quality. He is attracted to hard, massive, inhuman things, such as the deserted area of the Boulevard Noir. He dreams of losing his sensation of lymph, blood, and flesh and being nothing but *cold*.

Another aspect of his facticity is the past. As he tries to finish the biography of Rollebon, he wonders what the historical past consists of. The more he bends over it, the less he understands it. Not only are there mysteries and gaps in facts, which he cannot fill; the past simply will not let itself be grasped. This is because it *exists* no longer; it is only what has been; it is dead. History is reconstruction and invention, for there is nothing *behind* appearances. He finally realizes that he is pursuing chimera. M. de Rollebon dies a second time, "killed" or relegated to the past that he is. Roquentin's personal past is a little more tenacious, as represented by Anny especially. First, meditating on his reasons for leaving Indochina suddenly years ago, he realizes that then, as now, he was completely free, and that what seemed like a capricious act was simply the recognition that his past with its commitments and its "passion" was meaningless: he was already ahead of it. Then the Autodidact asks to see souvenirs of his travels and hear about his adventures. Watching him finger his souvenir postcards, Roquentin realizes that his own past is dead, as separate from him as the photographs. Furthermore, he has not had any adventures, if the word is understood properly. This is because adventures cannot take place in human temporality, which is always pro-jected forward. They are identified only in retrospect, from the far end, as something with inner necessity and a rare, precious quality, that happens according to a pattern, with a beginning, middle, and end. Human temporality has no beginning—it is always with us, since we *are* it—and no end except in death. Since the function of a moment in our whole lifetime cannot yet be known, it is impossible to live as if we were remembering, seeing our existence as a meaningful, necessary pattern; or rather, to do so is to be in bad faith. Furthermore, the sense of drama which accompanies some moments is simply the sense of time and its potentiality; what is being done during these moments is in no way special. People are misled by the apparent inevitability of happenings, like the turning up of a card in a game. This is erroneous: just because time is irreversible does not mean that its content is predestined, inevitable; it is an order that has no meaning. Adventures happen only in books, and books are narrated backwards; that is, the beginning of the story is chosen by the author in function of the end to which it must lead. The aesthetic perspective, which Anny used to practice by trying to make life a series of perfect moments, is to be condemned.

In Anny, who writes to him after several years' separation, Roquentin hopes to find refuge from his nausea and a justification which his historical research no longer affords. His trip to Paris to see her, from which he expects so much, is a failure. The past is dead, and Anny refuses to let him try to resurrect it. She too is disillusioned, and when he attempts to persuade her that they have changed together, she refuses to accept the resemblance: disillusionment cannot be a basis for a love that would deny it.

Roquentin likewise reflects on the future, which at times he seems to sense before it comes, as if an action (such as that of an old lady turning a corner) were spread out eternally and eternity were present. The future *is* present in a sense, as our possibility, our project always thrusting forward. Time is merely a mode of our existence, not something we are *in*. Various other idols also fall to his scrutiny. Knowledge, illustrated by the Autodidact, who is reading all the books in the library in alphabetical order, is a form of the project to *be*. The assimilation metaphor in *L'Etre et le néant* is suitable here: the Autodidact wishes to digest all the learning of the world, as if its secrets would then transform him into a special person, solid and real. He is also a humanist, of the Socialist variety. During a lunch to which he invites Roquentin—one of the comic highlights of the novel—the latter has to listen to his profession of faith in men, whom he claims to love (but very abstractly, since he too is a loner). Unfortunately, humanity in the abstract does not exist, any more than love or justice; everyone is equally empty on the inside, and the poor Autodidact is deceiving himself, spewing commonplaces of humanism in the conviction that ready-made values can give value to his life. It is wryly appropriate that his love for men should take the form of a barely exercised pederasty, and that in a final half-humorous, half-pathetic episode he should be ejected from the library. (Sartre will explore elsewhere the psychology of the homosexual, a particular form of bad faith.)

These experiences lead Roquentin to realize that there is nothing absolute, inherently ordered, or meaningful in human existence; there are no values except those created by men, and sentiments do not exist. As Anny says, one cannot find a great love; there is only I who love, and great loves must be created. One of his favorite topics is self-ascribed rights, which characterize the propertied classes: the right to ownership, to respect, to conjugal love, to final immortalization—all of which hide their ontological nothingness but cause shame in others and thus objectify them. His situation as an outsider helps him take cognizance of the bad faith of the bourgeois, with whom he refuses to identify although, with his independent income, he lives like one. In the splendid episode of Tourne-bride Street on Sunday, he observes the various subspecies of the middle class, their mechanical and artificial quality, the alienation of their speech and gestures from meaning, the relationships between the sexes and groups, and especially their obvious conviction that privilege and respect are their right.[5] This is what Sartre calls role-playing. Inside, they know they are not what they are; but they assume the role, a little too much, and pretend to convince themselves. They are *par excellence* the *others*—to him, to each other. He draws pleasure from dominating them by his height and his scorn, thus objectifying them. In the museum, he studies the portraits of dead members of the reigning families of Bouville, to whom his relationship is ambiguous. In one sense, he can dominate them all, for they are dead: their project is completely fixed as in-itself, with no more freedom. He takes particular delight in recalling the depths of hypocrisy and self-righteousness revealed by their biographies, which he has read in the library. However, in other ways the bourgeois dominate him. They incarnate the rights of the privileged classes. Furthermore, as Sartre shows in *L'Imaginaire,* the work of art is a special sort of image, with its own unreal existence; the burghers in the portraits no longer exist as men but exist (unreally) as portraits, with a solidity which is that both of the physical object (frame, paint, canvas) and the ideal artistic transcendence, to which the physical object points.[6] Roquentin cannot overcome this aspect of their transcendence; until he manages to see them as just flesh, the eyes of the figures stare down at him and seem to judge him, deny him the right to exist, penetrate to the heart of his nothingness. This is the effect of others' judgment, which, in his isolation, he usually avoids. His

parting shot, "Bastards," is only half-successful at exorcizing the fascination and shame he feels. But at least he knows they were in bad faith,
despite their claims on him and others.

In another scene, Roquentin observes one of the incarnations of class
rights, Dr. Rogé. A funny man named Achille has been condescending to
the waitress in a café, attempting thus to objectify her. Then Dr. Rogé, an
eminent representative of the bourgeoisie, aging but respected, enters.
Seeing Achille, he immediately puts him in his place by exclaiming, "You
old swine . . . aren't you dead yet?" (66). Instead of becoming angry,
Achille smiles and basks in the doctor's judgment. This is because he has
been classified, identified, and thereby given a being (even if a shameful
one) in the eyes of another, whom he recognizes as having the right to
judge. Roquentin is ashamed for him. He refuses to join in the doctor's
judgment; instead, he beats him at the staring-down game and comes to
see him for what he is: a big bag of ruddy flesh on spindly legs, whose
experience and rights do not change the fact that he will shortly die.

Roquentin's relationship with embodiment is elaborated as he is more
and more possessed by his nausea. For instance, he is aware of the saliva in
his mouth, a little pool that constantly forms, like thought, continuously
spinning out, no matter what one does. It is sweetish and almost viscous.
He is repulsed by food, a topic on which Sartre wrote some exceptionally
interesting pages (see *WS*, 61; *C*, 421–24). Why eat? To work? But why
work? To buy food? To keep existing? But why exist? To create more
existence—do things, beget children? There is no reason to do so; every
existant refers only to another for its justification, no one is indispensable
or necessary, and the system is circular. When the hero lunches with the
Autodidact, the chicken swimming in brown liquid looks disgusting. (He
also kills a fly, ridding it of existence.) Elsewhere, he sees the sausages in a
delicatessen not as cooked and edible, but as dead flesh; a hardboiled egg
with a drop of blood on it disgusts him.[7] In an erotic dream he sees a
garden, with hairy trees and horrible beasts, which smells of vomit and is
associated with food. Later he imagines trees transformed into phalluses.
In two episodes sexuality is connected especially with the conflict of
consciousnesses. In the park, Roquentin notices an exhibitionist, still
covered by his cape, staring at a little girl, who is fascinated by his gaze.
They form a couple, the dominant and the dominated. Roquentin too is
fascinated; he makes no attempt to interrupt the scene. But suddenly the
man sees Roquentin looking at him; he is then in his turn transformed
from subject into object, and his gaze loses its hold over the girl, who flees.
Later, Roquentin reads in the paper that the raped body of little Lucienne

has been discovered. What follows is one of the most interesting pages of the novel, in which surrealistic techniques are used in a stream-of-consciousness meditation to convey the pull of being in-itself, yet the constant freedom of the for-itself. Roquentin crumples the paper with his tensed fingers (like Lucienne's); he identifies strongly with the rapist, who might be the exhibitionist. He imagines the flesh of the girl, what it would be like to violate (and thus objectify) it; this is the sadistic impulse. It gives him a sense of being as in-itself, to which all human existence aspires. The idea of her *dead* body attracts him: it has become pure matter, and her thought exists no longer. He then replaces the pronoun *I* by *he* and switches to the masochistic position—what it would be like to be violated. Although it is physical, rape as a violation from behind is associated with thought, because thought constantly comes from behind. This episode contributes to an increasingly acute sense of existence as something Roquentin is surrounded by; "I think, therefore I am" is embedded in his monologue on the existence of papers, mud, bodies, the rights of the bourgeoisie, and he sees existence as a flaw, a "fall."[8]

Roquentin is also very much afraid of death, which since he has nothing to live for may seem paradoxical. Imagining a café owner lying in bed on a foggy day, perhaps dead, he pictures death so strongly that he flees through the streets. He is given to paranoia, which in another novel would be only a psychological quirk but in *La Nausée* has ontological implications: one's fear is a reaction to the realization of total liberty, in a world where anything can happen.

What remains after Roquentin has, one by one, broken the idols by which people deceive themselves is the recognition of brute existence. After lunch with the Autodidact has ended badly (Roquentin gets a terrific attack of nausea and tells his host there is no reason at all to exist), he walks along the seawall, takes a pointless tramway ride, and ends up in the park, scene of many a Sartrean meditation. At the beach he reflects on the ocean. It has been humanized by tradition, described, classified, poeticized. But its existence goes beyond all these anthropomorphic views, which do not even touch it.[9] On the streetcar he feels the metamorphosis of things, as they lose their name (seat) and function (something to sit on) and become brute, raw stuff, like a dead, sodden donkey. In the park, in the famous chestnut tree meditation, he sees that this stuff *is* existence. It is abundant, mouldy, and obscene, sticky, gelatinous, an "ignoble marmelade."[10] Human categories constantly cover it: order, groups, qualities, functions, potentialities. But none of these abstractions is in nature. A seagull is not "a type of shore bird" but rather a "seagull-existant." Language itself is an artificial construct imposed by man to make a world out of brute being; when the word "refuses to stick to the thing," as he says, one no longer comprehends it at all. The chestnut root is normally seen in its botanical function, and as black. But it is not pure black (an abstraction) but rather has a peculiar in-between appearance which escapes him, and, separated from its practical purpose, it is a senseless mass. Like all existence, it is below all explanation; explanations are a human invention, superimposed. He is nearly suffocated by this evidence. He realizes that all existants are *absurd*—not in relation to something (as a lunatic's ravings with respect to his real situation), but absolutely absurd. Human kind is not excepted from this universal absurdity. To it he applies the terms *de trop* (in the way, superfluous), contingent, and gratuitous. Existence cannot be deduced. One can ask neither about its beginning nor its end: these are strictly human points of view. Movement itself is not in nature, which is not going anywhere. There is no refuge from this absurdity. The Autodidact with his humanism, the bourgeois with their self-righteousness are as empty inside as he. "Every existing thing is born without reason, prolongs itself out of weakness and dies by chance" (133). Consciousness is what makes him aware of this. "If I exist, it is because I am horrified at existing" (99–100).

In this episode, the most crucial and one of the most dramatic of the novel, Roquentin has found out what he wanted to know. Although not all the distinctions made later in *L'Etre et le néant* are yet visible, the heart of Sartrean ontology can be derived from this passage. He now knows he is totally free, not only socially but ontologically, since there is no reason for or against anything, no absolute order. As he had seen, he could just as well stick his knife in the Autodidact's eye as cut his cheese with it. Even nature is "free," that is, has no built-in order and does not follow laws, which are derived by men as a simplification and a convenience. Anything can happen: a tongue can turn into a centipede; one might grow a third eye. Under the surface of the sea, which seems benign, perhaps a great monster is wallowing in the slime.

What is left, after such a devastating discovery? Suicide would be logical, even though it too would be superfluous, since it would be a new happening and there is absolutely no reason for a new happening. And Roquentin is afraid of death. But he must do something. Throughout the diary, he has had glimpses of a possible transcendence: art. Numerous specimens of art have been mentioned: a Khmer sculpture, a statue, the portraits, novels (Balzac's *Eugénie Grandet* is quoted extensively), and songs. Art objects are not of the domain of existence; they are ideal, unreally existent, like images. A jazz song, for instance, goes beyond its material realization; one can break the record but cannot lose the song, which he compares to a circle. The circle is an idea (the rotation of a line around one of its extremities). The song has a beginning, middle, and end, and true necessity, each part belonging to the whole in a set of unchanging relationships. Before leaving Bouville permanently, Roquentin goes to his favorite café and listens to "Some of These Days." It is noteworthy that the song speaks of the future, since man *is* his future in the mode of what he is not yet. "Some of these days / You'll miss me, honey." But the time of the art object is not ordinary time; it has its own transcendent time, which cannot be interrupted and cuts through ours. He thinks of the Jew who wrote the song and the Negress who sings it, two semipariahs, like him, who redeemed something of themselves by participating in the transcendence of the song. He is ashamed, and realizes that all along he too has wanted to *be,* to "drive existence out of me, rid the passing moments of their fat . . . purify myself, harden myself." He glimpses what could be the solution for him—to write another book, not a biography, since "an existant can never justify the existence of another existant," but a novel, which would be "beautiful and hard," above existence, and would make people ashamed to live. Then a little light would be shed on his past, and he could, like the composer and singer, who as much as possible have "washed themselves of the sin of existing," justify his existence a little and come to accept himself "in the past" (175–78).

The aesthetic solution foreseen here may seem surprising. It is, however, consistent with all Sartre's youthful ambition and the way he saw himself until the crisis of the 1950s (see *C,* 200). Whereas an identification between the author and his hero is often very false, in this case there is evidence that Roquentin's experiences, conclusions, and final redeeming project were indeed Sartre's. "At the age of thirty, I executed the masterstroke of writing in *Nausea*—quite sincerely, believe me—about the bitter unjustified existence of my fellow men and of exonerating my own. I *was* Roquentin; I used him to show, without complacency, the texture of my life" (*W,* 157–58; Sartre's emphasis). This is reflected in the hero's sense of superiority over his fellows, although, according to his own insights, there is no justification for such a posture: unlike the others he knows he exists without a reason. Thus the traditional French value of lucidity, cultivated by writers as various as Stendhal, Gide, Valéry, and Camus, asserts itself in a text which is nonetheless in some ways nauseous. Perhaps this helps explain how this novel, with its somber tone, its unpleasant treatment of the body, and its pessimistic view of man, can nevertheless be in other ways a very comic work.

Roquentin's project recalls Proust's effort to redeem the past by transforming it into a work of art through aesthetic vision, based on intuition and metaphor. However, the Proustian narrator's subject *is* explicitly his past. It is not clear that Roquentin intends to do an autobiographic work, still less clear that the diary itself is his novel. In any case, though the text is finished by Sartre, we do not know whether Roquentin ever started his book; these notes seem to be all that has remained of his attempt to overcome the contingency of facticity and achieve a justified being.

Le Mur

The collected stories in *Le Mur* take their title from the first, one of the best. All are ironic, that is, self-qualified. The characters are placed in revealing, sometimes extreme situations, up against the wall of circumstances or themselves. In the first case the wall is an actual one against which the Republican fighters are being executed by Spanish phalangists during the civil war. Here Sartre first reveals his fondness for situations in which men have to choose between life and death, indemnity and torture—situations which, like Karl Jaspers, he terms borderline or limit because they place man at the extreme point of the human condition and make his choices truly significant.[11]

"Le Mur," one of the best pieces of fiction concerning the Spanish Civil War, published first in 1937, was inspired when a former student came to ask Sartre for help in reaching Spain in order to fight on the Republican side (*WS*, 49). A tightly knit story in which character and circumstance are closely interdependent, it is Hemingway-like in the sober, concise style, the tendency toward understatement, and especially the ethos of the hero, who admires Ramon Gris because he is "hard" and who wants to "die cleanly," in contrast to the weakness shown by the two other captives.[12] Yet this is not simply another case of masculine pride facing tests of courage. It is so Sartrean that it can almost serve as a primer of his early philosophy.

The story is told in the first person, by the hero, Pablo. In the cellar where he and other prisoners await dawn, when they will be shot, he examines his fellows, the guards, a condescending doctor who has been sent to observe them, and himself. His situation is totally different from what it was: death, the end of possibility, removes the future and thus the temporal project which is man. Death is unnatural. Neither his present nor his past has any meaning: he cannot think of his girlfriend with warmth, and his memories are colorless. He is near that point when total facticity will take over. Objects such as a bench seem to have lost their solidity: consciousness is ontologically feeble and its intended objects likewise. He easily sees through the sham of the phalangists' seriousness, self-importance, and role-playing. He plays the staring-down game with the doctor until he realizes it no longer interests him; others have lost their importance, and he is concerned only with his own reactions. He is particularly aware of his own body, from which he feels alienated, and of other "bodies dying in agony while yet alive" (8). Flesh, especially that of the rather plump Tom, becomes pure obscene matter, without the freedom and project which transcend it; it is compared to butter, and expressed by animal metaphors. In the emotions of the men—their fear and the pity he almost feels for the youngest captive—Pablo seems to sense the defeat of freedom, the "magic" which arises when circumstances are overwhelming. When the officers ask him to reveal the hiding place of the Republican leader Gris, in return for his life, he invents one, not to save his life (from which he already feels separated) but as a game of the absurd, to see them go after a false lead—a gesture to the absurdity of all enterprise. The ending has an ironic O. Henry twist: by chance, Gris had fled to the very spot Pablo mentioned, where he is caught and shot. When Pablo learns, hours later, that he is still alive because the information he gave was correct, he responds with uncontrollable laughter. Though the neat ending may seem forced to some readers, it underscores the total contingency of situation: there is no meaning, no value in the world.

"La Chambre" ("The Room"), in two parts, is not so fine a specimen of the short story, either by its construction or its depiction of character. It is also less appealing because of its specialized topics, hallucinations and psychoses, which Sartre studied in the 1930s as phenomena of the imagination. It conveys less man's condition than his aberrations. But aberrations, Sartre would observe, are revealing. And the story also illustrates well the difficulties of relationships with others, as well as the theme of sequestration, recurrent in Sartre's work. The narrative point of view is neutral omniscience. The reader first shares the thoughts of Mme Darbedat (who caresses her memories and is as fleshy as Turkish paste[13]) concerning her daughter Eve and her insane son-in-law Pierre; next the point of view of the father, who is trying to convince Eve to have the deranged man committed; finally, that of Eve, who still loves her husband, confined behind the real and metaphorical walls of his lunacy. Sartre explores the relationships between the spouses, the husband's paranoia, and the wife's attempt, which foreshadows the behavior of the female characters in *Les Séquestrés d'Altona,* to reproduce by imagination the hallucinations he *really* has. Throughout the reader is aware of facticity, in Mme Darbedat's identification with her past and her soft flesh, M. Darbedat's red neck and sense of his own healthy body, and Pierre's strange attitude toward bodies. The in-itself is threatening: Pierre has an odd relationship to his fork, the light, the room, which he has possessed to the extent that Eve's belongings are alienated from her. The role of others is aggressive: by their looks, their judgments, they violate one's subjectivity and, as Eve says, drag it through the streets. Eve succeeds too well in entering his insane world. Words are losing their meaning, and she and Pierre are both tending toward solipsism, willing a kind of death of consciousness by the magic of emotion (fear) and the unreality of the imagination.

"Erostrate" ("Erostratus") is among the works which have given Sartre's fiction the reputation of being sordid and crude. No one who has proclaimed such hatred as he for the middle class and its values can be free of the suspicion of wanting to shock the reader. But the crudity here concerning sex and the body generally is not gratuitous, but rather reveals concepts basic in Sartrean philosophy: the obscenity of the body, sadism, and the desire to escape facticity. The principal character, who relates the story in the first person, hates all his fellows and despises the humanistic self-deceit which ascribes value to human beings in themselves. He wants to dominate others and thus prefers to look at their backs or heads, chiefly from several stories high (cf. *W,* 38). Their flesh disgusts him; he once faints at seeing a bloody, dead body. True, he hires prostitutes, but instead of making love to them gets his pleasure from observing them nude, that is, humiliating them in their fleshiest state. His project is to commit a memorable act of destruction, like that of Erostratus, famous for burning down the temple at Ephesus. It will be *hard,* self-caused and self-grounded, an acting out of freedom, thus the opposite of embodiment. He chooses a revolver, which he carries around lovingly, and prepares ceremoniously to shoot six people in the street.[14] The only difficulty is that, once posted and waiting for his victims, he cannot act, not from ordinary fear but because the passers-by seem to him already dead, emptied of meaning. He finally follows a big red-necked man whose flesh both repels and attracts him, and wastes three bullets shooting him, then two more firing into the crowd. The story ends as, cornered in a restaurant toilet, he throws away his gun (feeling powerless to shoot himself) and opens the door. Like Pablo, he commits an absurd act, in the face of the absurdity of all projects, and ironically survives it: not even destruction is meaningful or substantial; it too is a human project.

In "Intimité" ("Intimacy"), a story in six parts, Sartre is again concerned with human relationships, attitudes toward corporality, and bad faith. The situation is a cliché: an unhappy wife leaves her husband, only to return a day later, unable to live with the consequences of her action. While the role of others seems influential, it is the woman's own choice, freely made. Sartre uses both neutral omniscience and interior monologue in order to convey the points of view of the heroine, Lulu, and her friend Rirette, which correct each other. Despite her dissatisfaction, Lulu is tied to her impotent husband, Henri, whom she chose because he was "soft," like a priest. Her dreams of departing with her lover Pierre not only are extremely shallow escapist visions; in truth, his normal body with its normal desires disgusts her, and she feels dominated by his sexual confidence. She is thus in bad faith. The reader senses that she will return ultimately because Henri is not given to what Sartre elsewhere calls "nocturnal crudities" (*W*, 9). This enables her to dominate his "captive flesh" (56); she dreams of caring for him like a child. It also allows her to minimize her own facticity. "Why must we have bodies?" she exclaims, with respect to intercourse (60). Her attitude recalls puritanical Protestantism, but is present also in French Catholic literature.[15] Rirette, who more than Pierre is Henri's rival, tries to arrange her friend's adventure for her; it gives her vicarious romantic satisfaction and lets her dominate others, since they will owe their happiness to her. Her manipulations fail. First, she feels left out, as Lulu, having abandoned Henri for the moment, spends the evening with her lover; Rirette is the unwanted third. Then, Lulu returns home, and even Pierre is relieved; so that Rirette's interventions were not really desired. At the end, she is "flooded with bitter regret" (83).

The story is characterized by typically Sartrean features, including expressions of facticity by animal metaphors, the association of an empty-headed feeling (when consciousness is diminished) with stickiness, voyeurism, the role of others' thoughts as a violation of us, and the fear of being seen from behind (Lulu is even ashamed of having a *derrière*). It illustrates the conflict at the base of all human relations, the failure of pitiful attempts to get out of the subject-object dilemma, the captivity to flesh, and the failure of fantasy, as well as human responsibility for these failures.

"L'Enfance d'un chef," a long story or novella, is composed from the limited omniscient viewpoint. *Les Mots* reveals that Sartre borrowed many details in it from his own childhood, in the realm of affectivity more than fact. His aim, however, is not to depict himself, but to show how a Fascist temperament can be created by a middle-class upbringing, and how this satisfies the need of the for-itself for solidity and identity. The work can serve, among other things, as an example of how not to raise one's children; it is also a condemnation of French bourgeois society.

All Lucien Fleurier's youth illustrates the fundamental project of the for-itself to be, to overcome the freedom and nothingness of consciousness. As a child, he feels empty, incomplete, even nonexistent, because he has no essence, whereas those around him appear to. If it were not for their words, he would doubt he was real. He sees himself as adults see him, drawing his identity from them, so that when he is dressed to look like a girl, he thinks he may really be one (cf. *W*, 65). Yet he cannot quite accept their labels; perhaps adults too are fake, playing roles, so that there is no reality and all are playactors (cf. *W*, 53). At the core of his childhood, in short, are problems of identity. His mind is frequently compared to fog and mist; he is in a perpetual state of somnolence. That his sexuality is involved is not surprising, since he has difficulty generally in accepting embodiment. He sometimes feels all sticky; he has reveries about his mother's ample pink flesh and imagines her transformed into a beast. He both recoils from and desires being called a bean-pole. The label bothers him because it says what he *is* and yet he does not feel he *is* anything; but, if people use the word sufficiently, they may convince him and he will come to believe in himself. He feels strange when he hears others talk about him. God, the supreme witness, unfortunately knows that Lucien is not quite solid, that his sentiments are not quite true, and thus gives no assurance. He has difficulty believing even in the exterior world. Perhaps the hot water bottle, like a human being, is playing a role. Meditating like Roquentin on a chestnut tree, he tries to get it to affirm its self-identity, but it is inert. Torture of grasshoppers helps bring about a sense of reality; he is already a sadist, trying to affirm his subjectivity by objectifying another. He also tries masochism, objectifying himself and wallowing in humiliation. Unfortunately, one cannot fool consciousness, because one *is* it.

As a student, Lucien seeks self-affirmation variously, through philosophy (his professor explains the cogito as "You exist because you doubt your existence" [100]), emulation of others, who seem to him hard as iron, comradeship, reveries of suicide, and Freudian psychology. By explaining one, complexes make one real; he is happy to be classified as an Oedipal-anal. He also dabbles in surrealism and reads Rimbaud. Sartre uses this classic malaise to illustrate his view of how a young man seeks a ready-made self. Lucien is dazzled by a pseudo-Surrealist poet, a dandy, whom he suspects of being a homosexual without admitting it to himself (bad faith). When he finally recognizes it, he wonders about himself and pictures himself judged as "that old fairy." At least the label would give him being. Again, homosexuality is a category of self-deception.

Lucien's father has tried to give him a sense of his future responsibilities as head of the family manufacturing company, using commonplace arguments that ownership is a responsibility, that without capitalism there would be no jobs for workers—part of the stock-in-trade of the bourgeoisie, who thereby persuades itself of its right to hold property and govern. Lucien has never been able to believe in himself as a future leader. He feels no rights whatsoever; his existence seems unjustified, scandalous. Only by imagining himself from the outside, or identifying with someone who seems solid, can he have a sense of being. In the end it is anti-Semitism and right-wing politics that allow him to overcome his sense of inadequacy. They furnish his permanent character, the form taken by his project to be. Why are Fascist beliefs, which Sartre condemns on grounds that they contradict the basic freedom of man, so satisfying to Lucien? Because they affirm his right to *be* in particular forms: to be French, to despise the Jews. This is proven by others' reactions to his outspoken position: he is recognized as an essence. He then adopts this recognition as his own. At the end, having made an anti-Semitic outburst at a party, instead of being condemned, he is received with consideration. He imagines a strong, muscular back incarnating this personal force and realizes it is *his* back: seeing himself from behind, he sees massive power, instead of feeling vulnerable. He looks forward to inheriting the factory, marrying a pure girl of the same class, and possessing her (in the proprietary sense), "respected to the very flesh, obeyed to the very bed" (144).

Lucien thus returns to his class, and this story, like the others, is ironic. It is an old plot, the young rebel who matures and returns to his inherited values. For all his emphasis on freedom, Sartre suggests in *Les Mots* that if circumstances had been different, he too would have ended up this way: "Had [my father] left me property, my childhood would have been changed. I would not be writing, since I would be someone else. House and field reflect back to the young heir a stable image of himself. . . . *I was not* substantial or permanent" (*W,* 55; Sartre's emphasis). The portraits in this story are particularly scathing, because he knew the bourgeoisie so well, notably his stepfather, because as a child he was sensitive to problems of identity and sincerity, and finally because of his arsenal of literary techniques: images, literary allusions, the telling single detail, and varying distance from his subject. This "sentimental education," in spite of some tediousness, is an outstanding illustration of how fiction can give life to philosophy.

Chapter Four

The Later Fiction

Introduction

In 1947 Sartre indicated his views on what postwar fiction should be, and although he did not specifically relate them to his current work, they are clearly applicable and can serve as an introduction as well as a standard by which to judge his novels of the 1940s.[1] His thesis was that the war had brought a radical change in men's perspective on history and themselves, such that they could no longer accept the suppositions of prewar fiction, especially its absolute stability. "We . . . involved in a system in full evolution, could know only relative moments." He wished, in other words, to "make the technique of the novel shift from Newtonian mechanics to generalized relativity." This implied the end of omniscient narrators or witnesses and privileged viewpoints, and their replacement by characters *in situation,* "whose reality would be the tangled and contradictory tissue of each one's evaluations of all the other characters. . . ." It meant the end of authorial judgment, replaced by readers' conclusions that would be only possibilities, not certainties. He wanted to end retrospective literature (which involves the taking of a position) and to restore to the event immediacy, ambiguity, unforeseeability, and "brutal freshness," avoiding the pastness of previous fiction. The reader is to experience *with* the characters. "Let every character be a trap, let the reader be caught in it, and let him be tossed from one consciousness to another . . . let him be uncertain [from] the very uncertainty of the heroes, disturbed by their disturbance, flooded with their present. . . ." Sartre names as his models Kafka and the American novelists. He wants to posit the a priori equivalence of all subjectivities and notes that one of the technical problems is "to find an orchestration of consciousnesses which may permit us to render the multidimensionality of the event." The reader is to enter each character's mind. Ultimately, Sartre wants fiction to project the reader forward, like a toboggan, and let the novel stand alone: "We want to drive providence from our works as we have driven it from our world." He also wishes to integrate things into the novel (and here he sounds very much like a phenomenologist) by the multiplicity of men's relationships with them: "The world and man reveal themselves by undertakings." This leads him to define his aim as a literature of praxis, "action in history and on history . . . a synthesis of historical relativity and moral and metaphysical absolute."[2] Whether his postwar fiction succeeds in renewing the novel to this extent can be considered only after one has read *Les Chemins de la liberté;* but knowing some of Sartre's views on fiction may help the reader understand the unusual techniques in his later novels, especially multiple plots, lack of transitions, and changing focus.

L'Age de raison

The first two parts of *Les Chemins de la liberté,* published in 1945, were conceived as early as 1938 and partly written before the outbreak of the war. While reflecting Sartrean phenomenology and ontology, they were intended as a step toward a more committed literature, which would present in aesthetic terms the doctrine of freedom and its consequences.[3] Sartre thought of the hero, Mathieu Delarue,[4] as a continuation of Roquentin who would progress beyond a negative position and its aesthetic solution to a stage of action and involvement with the world. With the war and the Occupation, Sartre's own changing attitude encouraged him to develop his hero's awareness of his time.

Although throughout the three volumes of *Les Chemins* and the unfinished fourth, there is considerable continuity of theme and character, each volume can be read separately. This autonomy, plus the short time period covered by the series, makes it different from the *roman fleuve* as practiced by Jules Romains, Martin du Gard, and others. The first volume, *L'Age de raison (The Age of Reason),* is conventional, less philosophic than *La Nausée,* with a wider range of characters and a more anecdotal plot. Using neutral omniscience, Sartre divides his material into chapters which focus on one or two characters, perhaps three, and one or two plot threads. Most of the narration is in the third person, but at times the author switches to first-person interior monologue to show the flow of consciousness. The action covers three nights and two days. The themes are divided among the characters, with an apparent attempt to keep Mathieu, a philosophy professor, from being the exclusive spokesman for Sartrean ideas. Dialogue, interior monologue, and the interconnecting plot threads are well handled. The latter all revolve around Mathieu, but auxiliary characters are allowed to develop independently also, for one of Sartre's aims is to present the mood of pre-1939 France, especially its complacency, irresponsibility, and historically ironic illusion (a type of inauthenticity) that destinies could be purely individual. The basic plot line can be stated as a question: will Marcelle, Mathieu's mistress, keep her child or have an abortion, and will Mathieu marry her or avoid this lien on his freedom? Although this is the stuff of cheap drama, Sartre uses it chiefly to support Mathieu's reflections on his freedom.

To this main plot are added others, concerning secondary characters, who reappear in later volumes. Mathieu's friend Daniel is obsessed with his own pederasty, guilt, and drive toward self-punishment, while nevertheless aspiring at times toward the lightness of pure consciousness. Sartre's excellent analysis, based on *L'Etre et le néant,* reveals a man who has chosen shame and who begs for others' judgment so that he may be given a definition, reduced to the thinglike state he craves, and thus freed from the burden of responsibility and guilt. Self-hatred is not sufficient since consciousness is always conscious of itself: he cannot objectify himself. But the hatred of another is more effective. If others can see him as a homosexual, he can perhaps accept himself as being one. He also yearns to be another and identifies strongly with Marcelle, to the point of feeling her humiliation. This masochistic impulse, which prompts his confession to Mathieu, is, like his homosexuality, a type of bad faith. It is paralleled by a sadistic desire to hurt and dominate people with whom he is involved because that too gives him a being. After his first two attempts at a conclusive masochistic act fail, a third try succeeds: he will marry Marcelle, whom he has charmed by his attentions and elegance but whom he despises, so that she may keep her baby and Mathieu will be humiliated, though free; he thus arranges for himself long-term misery, a bloodless suicide.

Among other characters who deserve mention is Ivich, an unhappy provincial girl supposedly studying science in Paris, with whom Mathieu is half in love but who scorns him as an adult, like her parents, the epitome of bourgeois respectability. Modeled on Olga Kosakiewicz, Sartre's friend of the 1930s, Ivich, though irritating, has a charm to which Mathieu responds. She refuses as much as possible the claims of flesh to eat and sleep—that is, facticity. Her brother Boris, Mathieu's former pupil and admirer, shares her total commitment to the present; he cannot even imagine the future. Sarah, a Jew, introduces the theme of Nazi persecutions, and thus gives a glimpse of the political background, ignored by those involved solely in their individual dramas. The mention of her husband, Gomez, a painter, who has been fighting on the Republican side in Spain, serves to remind Mathieu of the struggle against Fascism and his vague guilt because he did not volunteer. His Communist friend Brunet is the spokesman for an even more radical commitment, in which one renounces totally his freedom of action, and by this choice finds meaning in a life otherwise empty. Whereas Mathieu has lost, he says, the sense of reality, Brunet seems real, physically; he exudes solidity, meaning, discipline, a "healthy universe" removed from the nauseous and inauthentic concerns of Mathieu. His presence makes Mathieu feel at fault, a "dirty intellectual."[5] Although he is not yet the perfect model because he too has abdicated some responsibility by transferring his personal choices to the party authority, Brunet illustrates the relationship between ontological freedom and the imperative to struggle for a corresponding political freedom. A foil to Brunet is Mathieu's brother Jacques, a serious, class-conscious bourgeois lawyer.

Much of the text has a familiar phenomenological quality. Perspective and intention reveal reality differently to each character. Reflecting on Gauguin's paintings, Mathieu thinks, "Pictures . . . have no positive force, they are no more than suggestions; indeed, their existence depends on me, I am free as I confront them" (91). The characters feel themselves as project, from the inside, not as beings occupying civil and social status. Others always seem to them more solid and real. They play roles for each other, e.g., the bartender playing the role of a bartender, exaggerating to give himself the being he feels he does not have. People are "naturally bogus" (227). Consciousness is basic; it is transparency, void, nothingness, sticking to things, and is always conscious of itself, so that no true self-deceit is possible. Mathieu calls himself a bastard but knows he is not sincere; it is a trick to redeem himself, called "lucidity." "Suddenly, Mathieu began to open gently like a wound; he saw himself exposed and as he was: thoughts, thoughts about thoughts, thoughts about thoughts of thoughts, he was transparent and corrupt beyond any finite vision" (220). Thought is constantly moving ahead, and one cannot escape it. "He wishes he were dead, and he exists, he obstinately maintains his own existence" (357). He thinks of his unborn child as a consciousness, an image of the world that will never be. Existence is gratuitous, without justification. Imaginary elements are expressed as powerfully as perceptions, following Sartre's view that they occupy consciousness just as fully, if unreally. The literary image, often synesthetic, serves Sartre's purpose well, translating by language into a correlative mental image for the reader the characters' intentionality; like *La Nausée,* the text is almost poetic in spots. Sartre excells at rendering the feelings of the body—a hand touching cloth or skin, the ferruginous taste of existence in the mouth, a cottony feeling in the arm. Tactile images abound. The sense of the present is very strong; what is present *is* time, along with the past, which men reevaluate as they wish, and a future as yet unreal. Mathieu's meditation on Boris's seemingly dead mistress Lola shows how much human reality is associated with its future.

The principal theme of the novel is freedom. In a story where both character and circumstances seem at least as compelling as in most fiction, there is still a strong sense of human freedom, not to change external factors but to look at oneself and the world as one wishes, to decide on one's nature and interpret and evaluate what in itself has no given value. Mathieu is the chief illustration of this freedom, but for him it has been wholly negative. He has wanted to be without ties and to found all his acts in this freedom, keeping himself available for a radically new act which would begin a new existence. The other side of this freedom is solitude and responsibility: he can blame no one, he has chosen his own good and evil, "condemned forever to be free" (320). But the fundamental ontological freedom of *L'Etre et le néant* is translated into concrete terms: what does it mean to remain free, in France in 1938, for a professor with a pregnant mistress and insufficient funds for a safe abortion? His reflections lead to the ironic conclusion that he is free for nothing; unoriented, uncommitted freedom finally is meaningless. A glimmer of understanding comes when he tells himself that to want to be what he is the only freedom left to him, that is, to be Marcelle's companion by marrying her. But he cannot act on this, except as if by compulsion; his delayed offer of marriage is that of a desperate man. Even his tardy success at obtaining money is meaningless, for it is not wanted: Marcelle wishes to keep her baby, and Daniel's proposal means that no one has any more claims on Mathieu; the future seems emptied of possibility. "All I do, I do *for nothing*. It might be said that I am robbed of the consequences of my acts," he emphasizes (395). In different ways his friends all suggest that having freedom means choosing a course of action and following it. (Sartre gives to somewhat unlikeable characters the function of criticizing Mathieu's erroneous view, a technique repeated later.)

Another theme is the role of others. Relationships such as those of Boris and Lola, Mathieu and Marcelle, Mathieu and Ivich, Daniel and a male prostitute fail again and again; they are based on bad faith, deceit, and the ceaseless play of subject and object. The characters feel they exist for others, in their consciousness; this can be reassuring or humiliating.

People differ according to one's perspective on them: to Mathieu, Marcelle seems a quite different person when Daniel describes their clandestine encounters (in respect to which Mathieu plays the role of the unwelcome third). Love is experienced as an attempt to feel as the other without ceasing to be oneself. Verbal communication reveals the failure of relationships; it sometimes seems that exchanging words merely obscures understanding, and the more characters insist they are frank the more they dissimulate. One of the most enduring of literary themes, human misunderstanding, receives here a particularly Sartrean illustration.

Embodiment, a crucial aspect of facticity, stands in thematic contrast to freedom and is related to the theme of others. The clearest illustration of the pull of the body, as both a fascinating and a disturbing presence, is the nightclub episode in which first Ivich, then Mathieu stab their hands with Boris's knife.[6] It is less a matter of self-destruction than an effort to apprehend one's body from the outside—to take a point of view on it, as consciousness does *through* the body, on others. Similarly, in the episode where Boris thinks Lola is dead, the sense of a physical presence, all the stronger because there is no consciousness, is horrible to him. Perhaps the most interesting illustration of the malaise of facticity is Marcelle's pregnancy. To both Mathieu and Daniel, she is somewhat repulsive, occupied by a body growing within hers, which will be ultimately separate from her. Her consciousness seems imprisoned in her fertile, almost overripe flesh, and neither she nor the others can stop staring at her body. Yet to her, the foreign object within is something more; it will be, she hopes, the justification of her life, the fullness given to an empty existence.

Whether lover or café waiter, the characters are hypersensitive to another's gaze; it is sometimes enough to motivate them to act. The sense of being watched causes discomfort and shame, since it objectifies the person; Mathieu, for instance, feels naked under Brunet's look, which is a reproach for his refusal to commit himself, and when an older homosexual picking up a boy catches Daniel looking at him, he loses all his assurance. Boris is nervous as Lola watches him because her looks of love call for a response he is incapable of giving. Daniel comes to wish he could live among the blind. Yet the look can be comforting insofar as the person wants to be objectified by the judgment of others. Another frequent motif is the viscous—softness, sweetness, stickiness, found in the butterlike flesh of Marcelle and her vomit, the pasty feeling Boris gets when making love and the correlation between voice and a sugary taste in the mouth. These all reflect the malaise of consciousness in its embodiment, the fear of being swallowed by matter, which is neither a free-flowing stream nor a solid.

L'Age de raison is ultimately critical. Mathieu's one bold act—the theft of Lola's money—is stolen from him, and he is branded by Daniel a bastard. He is left alone, having reached the age of reason, but without passions or commitments, a picture of the unattached man, whose life is given him for nothing. Even if the road to freedom passes through the realization of complete ontological liberty, it cannot, the reader senses, end there.

Le Sursis

The second volume of the trilogy, *Le Sursis (The Reprieve)*, whose title throws an ironic light on the action, represents a new departure in Sartrean style.[7] Using techniques borrowed from Virginia Woolf and John Dos Passos, whom he admired greatly at the time, Sartre created an impressionistic picture of France in September 1938, at the time of the Munich agreement, as a collectivity, though composed of individuals living out their own dramas as well as Europe's. This is an early example of what he means by a detotalized totality, a concept crucial in his later writings. It echoes the Unanimists, who at the beginning of the century suggested that social groups were more than just the sum of their parts, that they had a collective soul, and who tried to invent literary techniques to convey this; there are also some points of contact with Zola. Since all Europeans are threatened by the impending invasion of Czechoslovakia, the unifying factor is war, present as a constant menace—almost the main character in the drama. War is an intention of consciousness and exists because and wherever one is conscious of it. Everyone is responsible for it because it is a collective project. Yet it is a detotalized totality. "War: everyone is free, and yet the die is cast. It is there, it is everywhere, it is the totality of all my thoughts, of all Hitler's words, of all Gomez's acts; but no one is there to add it up. It exists solely for God. But God does not exist. And yet the war exists."[8]

Among the numerous techniques used to re-create fictionally this collective experience, the most basic is multiple *dramatis personae*, locations, and plots. Whereas in most historical novels, a very few represent the fate of large numbers, here there are many characters, including those from *L'Age de raison*, plus new ones, from major historical figures—Hitler, Chamberlain, Daladier—to an illiterate shepherd. Most of them are ignorant of the others but their destinies are joined, above them, beyond their vision, by the threat of war. Perhaps the example of Malraux's *L'Espoir (Man's Hope)* was influential. A second technique is abrupt transitions, within paragraphs and even within sentences, often based on pivotal phrases or words which refer either backward or forward. The frequent change of pronoun antecedents without indication makes the text obscure, until other clues reveal the transitions. This procedure, while making a first reading discouraging, does contribute on subsequent readings to a sense of the copresence of the many characters, embracing also the reader. It is supported by parallelism of grammatical and episodic construction and by repetition. It also contributes to a third feature—simultaneity of action. While Hitler is conferring or speaking on the radio (whose waves serve as an image of the political threat over the continent), Boris is talking to Lola, Mathieu to his sister-in-law Odette, Ivich is with her father, and Milan and Anna are watching Germans occupy their Czech town. The imperfect tense is used to good effect to render this sense of simultaneous action. Another technical feature is the frequent use of interior monologue, sometimes lengthy, sometimes merely a brief first-person phrase. These techniques presuppose authorial omniscience, which is focused for only brief passages on one or two characters alone, ranging the rest of the time among the many plots and actors. It is this quasi-divine perspective, which violates the author's precept against assuming a god-like stance, which helps reveal the meaning of the novel. The viewpoint is highly visual, often cinematographic; yet there are still numerous tactile and gustative images which serve typically as correlations for consciousness.

The novel is divided into eight sections, corresponding to the eight days of the action. The political drama begins with a conversation between Chamberlain and Horace Wilson on 23 September and concludes with Daladier's return to Paris after the Munich pact and his famous remark upon being cheered by the crowd, "The God-damned fools!"[9] There is no need to review the numerous plots, mostly anecdotal rather than structural, often just vignettes, intended to show what Frenchmen were doing in 1938. The themes include those of the previous volume, plus others more explicitly political. Some of the most salient will be examined, in connection with the characters from whose actions they are derived.

The aspiration to freedom and its anguish are again represented by Mathieu. The chestnut tree episode of *La Nausée* has its parallel here in a long meditation on freedom during Mathieu's last hours in Paris. In anguish, he has become aware that he is absolutely free, gratuitous, fortuitous; the freedom he thought he had to search for was himself, all along. Around him, things are a plenitude. There is no reason for any act, no absolute law to follow; free for nothing, he is still forced to act. He considers throwing himself from the Pont Neuf; after all, he is free to do so. Suddenly, without justification, he decides not to. He has so little commitment to the present that he does not mind being called up; and when the peace agreement is signed, he decides that, whereas everyone else is going to return to things as they were, he will not resume the meaningless routine of the past; this decision suggests that he will now dispose of his life differently, *using* that gratuitous life for something that would give it meaning.

The difficulties of being a middle-class convert to a working-class political ethic—a theme in several other Sartrean works—are apparent in the comparison drawn between Brunet and Maurice, a Communist of proletarian origin. Maurice and Zézette incarnate the class struggle, and reveal how the bourgeoisie makes the lower classes feel vaguely guilty. Right-wing views are again presented by Jacques Delarue, who favors appeasement, fearing that war will lead to a proletarian revolution. Gros-Louis the shepherd, who does not even know he must report for military duty, represents the political victimization of the ignorant. Gomez again incarnates the authenticity of those who have chosen the cause of freedom and act on their choice. He is the spokesman for the view, proven true, that Czechoslovakia will not satisfy Hitler, and that to yield to his demands is simply to invite further aggression.

The theme of inauthenticity and the need for a mediator is illustrated brilliantly by Daniel, superficially devoted to Marcelle, strongly attracted to young men, suffering under his self-punishment and enjoying it, though wanting more. He wishes for war, which he calls a "sea of hatred" (47); he will enjoy seeing others' fear. A long letter to Mathieu, which reads like a lesson in the ontology of *L'Etre et le néant,* reveals that he has begun believing in God, not so that he may be forgiven, but so that he may be seen, known from the inside, and thus be what he is, coinciding with himself, the pure object of his hatred. God is the supreme witness, who sees not the "froth and foam of our daily thoughts" but the "eternal essence" of a man (408). Daniel changes the cogito, which depends on evasive, transparent thought, to "I am seen, therefore I am" (407). What does it matter that he is seen as guilty, as long as it gives him a being. This conversion is a form of the bad faith already exemplified by his cowardice and his homosexuality; for to rely on God for one's being is to renounce freedom while yet knowing that one is entirely free.

Among secondary themes are love, man as object, role-playing, and others. In the cases of Maurice, Gomez, and Irène (a working-class woman whom Mathieu meets), it is suggested that love can be authentic; or it can be inauthentic, as with Lola, hanging onto Boris, and Boris, who wishes so much to leave her that he volunteers for military service just as the Munich agreement is signed. Through the bed-ridden Charles, who is evacuated with others from his sanatorium at Berck because of the threat of war, Sartre explores the theme of man as object. He is marked by sexual passivity and the desire to *be* the object he is for others, yet resentment of those who walk, and desire for the war, which would level out these inequities by making everyone lie down, on the battlefield or in the grave. While the passages concerning Charles were criticized for their scatological and sexual features, the portrait is sympathetic, and the episode in which he is separated from the lovely invalid Catherine, the only creature who has ever made him feel like a man, is perhaps the most poignant of the book.[10] Philippe, an adolescent pacifist who resembles Baudelaire, is, like Daniel, a study in cowardice and role-playing.[11] His chief aim is to punish his mother for having remarried and insult his stepfather, a general; but though he forces himself in a spirit of martyrdom to cry "Down with war!" in the streets, he cannot leave for Switzerland with his fake passport because he lacks resolution, and perhaps because he needs the French as witnesses. The role of others is again crucial in consciousness of oneself. When he leaves home, Philippe's satisfaction comes from thinking how worried his mother is, how he now exists for her more solidly than when he was present. A number of Jewish characters introduce the theme of others, since they are, by definition, "others" within French society, though this does not correspond to an essence, as Sartre's famous definition shows: a Jew is a man whom others take for a Jew (96).[12]

Consciousness itself is sometimes a theme, more often the vehicle for others. Intentionality is primary; consciousness organizes the world. Imagining the sea in wartime, Mathieu realizes that it will no longer be the same sea; Paris is transformed as Mathieu and Ivich view it with the eyes of war. Viscosity and sweetness are again associated with consciousness, especially a bad conscience, and Ivich's loathing of the physiological recalls the burden of facticity. There is no transcendent self, just a series of little eccentric movements of consciousness, with horror at the center. Only death, represented by the corpse of Armand Viguier, gives solidity and definition to what is otherwise all porous. Consciousness is ubiquitous: Mathieu is at the same time in the train, on the beach, and in Berlin.

This is the philosophic justification for the technique of scene-switching and simultaneous action, as well as the notion of responsibility. Moreover, though individual, each consciousness is involved with millions of others over the world, as if in a giant multi-dimensional polyp. Destiny is the detotalized totality of these consciousnesses. All consciousness is temporal, and the sense of the changed future, the variable value of the past are very strong in *Le Sursis*. Without a future, action seems suspended, senseless; knowing what the future will be changes the sense of the past.

One of the major questions presented by the novel is the ethical one. Ontologically speaking, all acts are equal. Boris muses that, in a sense, everything has value: coffee in the trenches is as good as coffee in a station (337). Mathieu has no reason not to commit suicide. He tells Jacques that no matter how many people die in a war, humanity is always as full as before, and life is neither short nor long, but an ontological whole (210). Yet when the crowd is about to beat up Philippe for his pacifist provocations, Mathieu steps in to rescue him. What the relationship is between total ontological and ethical freedom, on the one hand, and its use for any cause, on the other, is not suggested, so that, like *L'Age de raison,* the novel ends critically and enigmatically: the French are fools for abandoning Czechoslovakia, yet according to Mathieu's understanding of liberty, there is no reason not to do so. This contradiction will concern Sartre in subsequent works.

La Mort dans l'âme

Entitled *Troubled Sleep* or *Iron in the Soul*[13] in translation, the third volume of the series, less of an artistic whole than the others, is in two parts, connected not by plot and characters but topically, through the main theme of war. The second part poses problems which are resolved only in the sequel and then only partly. While familiar phenomenological approaches are visible, politics and history dominate. It is a story of military debacle and defeat in June 1940. Less forceful artistically and less apocalyptic than Claude Simon's *La Route des Flandres (The Flanders Road),* to which it can be compared, it is more optimistic, suggesting that defeat and despair are nevertheless a way of constructing a new France.

In the first part, divided into sections dated 15 June through 18 June, major characters of previous volumes appear in the context of the defeat; Sartre thus reviews the circumstances of representative French at that date and shows their attitudes toward the war. The point of view is neutral omniscience, focused for long passages on one or two characters only, sometimes in the first person. Sartre makes less use of simultaneous narration than in *Le Sursis,* and there are many fewer abrupt transitions. Gomez appears first, in New York (portrayed unfavorably), where he is trying to find work as an art critic, since he no longer wants to paint; painting is too optimistic, and justifies suffering. Reading of the fall of Paris, he feels that in this land of optimists he is the only one concerned. Sartre introduces here the theme of political responsibility and guilt, which runs through the novel and is summarized in his phrase that men get the war they deserve.[14] Gomez's conclusion is even more pessimistic, however: his old belief in action for the cause of freedom is gone. Boris, shown recuperating from combat wounds in Marseilles, says his life ended at Sedan in May. However, a future *is* offered, in the form of flight to England and participation there in the continuing struggle, a choice which presents a typically existentialist dilemma: go, and make Lola unhappy, or stay out of loyalty to her and forego the chance to give his life meaning.

The second and fourth sections show Mathieu and seven companions in a French village, where their officers have abandoned them in utter disorder, after retreating. They believe mistakenly that the armistice has already been signed. The theme of responsibility is echoed: "There were eight of them there who had lost the war" (44). That they had no chance to fight, but only to retreat, does not matter; they are guilty not only in 1940 but before all future generations. The defeat makes Mathieu conscious of his nationality for the first time, since being French seems no longer an absolute, a given; it is an accident, like life itself. Characteristic Sartrean impressions of time make this moment appear less as one in a historical process of cause and effect than timeless, suspended. This is partly because the war, virtually over, has fallen into the past, in-itself; it is no longer a project and there is none to replace it, except "local moments" (121). The frequent Sartrean sense of *taedium vitae* is very strong. Impressions of phenomena are rendered in part through organic images: the men are vermin, blamed by everyone (125); Mathieu feels the objective independence of the world with respect to him, despite his consciousness, as "this flat forest of living things" which "would still be there when they were dead" (172).

Subsequent sections focus on Daniel and Mathieu, in different settings of defeat. The former is wandering in Paris, deserted and gloomy to a patriot but exhilarating to him, since he hopes the German occupants will destroy the city. It is no surprise that this cowardly pederast should also be a traitor: it is another mode of his bad faith. He feels German eyes on him everywhere. The soldiers attract him physically and morally; they are the avenging gods sent to strike French middle-class morality; they are the other to whom he will be subservient in a masochistic relationship, while sadistically rejoicing in France's chastisement. By the Seine, he meets a youth about to jump in, and entices him to go home with him. This is Philippe, who has deserted from the disorganized army, returned to Paris to see his mother, and, not finding her, wants to kill himself because he cannot live with his cowardice, and fears the general's judgment. Daniel proposes to reeducate him completely, first by liquidating all his assumptions and teaching him to love his new masters, the Germans. Meanwhile, Mathieu, demoralized, finds that he cannot react as the other soldiers do, by getting disgustingly drunk. (The vulgarity of their dialogue is accentuated in the English translation.) Annoyed because he seems to judge them, without wanting to, and because they resent his attitude, Mathieu suffers at the picture of their humiliation and wants to become one of them. A buddy, Pinette, proposes that Mathieu accompany him to a nearby village as yet untaken, where a stray outfit is going to try to hold off the Germans. This is pointless, Mathieu argues; he will just get himself killed. Yet he finally takes a rifle and follows, a gratuitous decision which reveals a change in him: he has no good reason to do so, has a good reason not to, and yet chooses to commit himself to an action which will thereby have meaning for him.

The first part ends with the most memorable sequence of the volume. Mathieu and Pinette join the strays on the roof of the church belfry, and with difficulty establish some comradeship. Examining his conscience, he decides that whether or not he has a "right" to leave his former buddies and die here for nothing is for him only to decide—that no one can judge him and that he is through with scruples, ready to commit himself and die, thus extinguishing the earth. For fifteen minutes he succeeds in holding out, in a euphoric state of freedom and power.[15] Although this may appear to be an illustration of Sartre's views of freedom and action, Mathieu is involved in a purely negative act; when he shoots defiantly, he resembles a rebellious adolescent. "He was firing on his fellow men, on Virtue, on the whole world: Liberty is Terror" (255–56). Sartre later remarked that Mathieu was the negation of true freedom (*WS*, 115).

Part two concerns Brunet, surrendering when he sees that further resistance is useless, straggling along the roads with other prisoners, then in a prison camp, finally in a freight car. Developed by contrasts with that of other prisoners, especially one called Schneider, very sympathetically portrayed, his character is mainly a function of politics: he thinks *for* the party. Much of the discussion centers directly on how, through discipline, a Communist core can be built among the captives, and how this is necessary for the long struggle—not so much against the Nazis as against France and themselves, with their complacency, petty ambitions and satisfactions, and lack of resolve. Other passages concern the responsibility for the defeat and the expediency of the Nazi-Soviet pact of August 1939. Schneider, who says he is a party sympathizer, criticizes the pact on grounds both of practicality and principle. (He can be identified partly with Paul Nizan, whom Sartre defended posthumously against Communist charges of treason.[16]) Brunet argues that a party decision cannot be questioned; moreover, it was the most opportune move, and ultimately the USSR will intervene because the Russian proletariat will never abandon its Western brethren. Meanwhile, he attempts to form the Communist prisoners into a cell. His success is not far-reaching, for once they are fed, the men are not dissatisfied enough, and clutch at the hope of returning home. This hope is Brunet's greatest enemy. In the last pages, crowded into boxcars, the men are sure they are being shipped to Châlons. Brunet suspects and (as Schneider guesses) hopes otherwise, for only by recognizing the Germans as enemies, by feeling crushed, beaten, and mistreated, will they have enough spirit to affirm their solidarity with others and accept discipline. When the westbound train takes a spur track to the north, toward Luxembourg and Germany, and the German guards, having shot one escapee, close the doors to prevent further attempts, Brunet feels at last that they have sunk into darkness and that he will be able to work. Brunet's dogmatism is an intellectual form of the fatuity that marks some of his crude companions. Sartre called him the embodiment of the spirit of seriousness, which believes in transcendent values written in the sky, and is not free (*WS,* 115). However, he does represent the Sartrean political position that capitalist society must be destroyed and a socialist France take its place.

To these political matters are added many observations, of which only a sampling from both parts can be given: the speed with which the past moves away (like a moving train), a corpse as in-itself, the alienation of the body, the force of imagination (Boris feels he is already in England), anger as a way of escape, and the power of the gaze. The Sartrean brand is everywhere; still, the volume's conventionality and primary concern with war and defeat make it the least ontological of the trilogy and indicate the author's increasingly political orientation.

"Drôle d'amitié"

"Drôle d'amitié" (Strange friendship) is, except for recent posthumous fragments, the only published portion of the conclusion of the series, which would probably have been called *La Dernière Chance,* in which Sartre lost interest and which he chose not to complete.[17] Although a fragment, it can stand by itself artistically and reads like a novella. It is both an adventure story and an ideological one. Long discussions of the Communist position during the period between the Nazi-Soviet pact and Russia's entry into the war will seem tedious to some, but the element of suspense helps outweigh that flaw. The point of view is limited omniscience, focused on the mind of Brunet. The third person is used almost entirely; occasionally a first-person phrase of interior monologue brings Brunet's consciousness closer to the reader. Dialogue predominates, and Sartre renders well the slang and popular speech of the prisoners.

Every concern in this work is political, since each is seen through Brunet's eyes and, as a self-appointed Communist leader in the prison camp where the action takes place, he aims at teaching that no act is neutral and all the worker's life must be politicized, oriented toward achieving the revolution. Schneider has helped Brunet form groups of Communists and sympathizers. The action is set in motion when a newly arrived party member, Chalais, recognizes in Schneider the journalist Vicarios, a loyal Communist until 1939, when he denounced the Nazi-Soviet pact and was branded a traitor. Brunet's orthodoxy obliges him to break with Schneider, for whom his friendship has been ambivalent anyway. This is one of the crises of the fragment, a personal as well as political one. A more severe conflict takes place within Brunet himself when Chalais informs him that the party line is now one of cooperation with the German conquerors. Objectively, Brunet's camp propaganda is playing into the hands of the Gaullists and thus capitalism. All his anti-German teaching now has to be undone. His recognition of absolute party authority requires him to accept this antinationalist line and confess his error publicly; yet he cannot cease hoping the Soviets will declare war and destroy Fascism. In a dramatic reversal, his situation thus resembles Schneider's, but he struggles against admitting that his friend was right.

When a few party members learn of Schneider's identity and, indoctrinated by Chalais, beat him up, Brunet finds himself defending him, thus objectively acting as a traitor himself. Friendship alone would not suffice to provoke this change; it comes from the dread that if the USSR ever joins the war it will be defeated, thus dooming the cause of men everywhere. Schneider has long wished for the time when other party leaders would be in his position—ostracized and suffering internal conflict; he has hated them, rather than hate himself.[18] Yet he now feels no satisfaction upon seeing Brunet in the same position.

After this ideological change, Brunet consents to help Schneider escape and resolves to join him. Their perception of the wind, the darkness, the disguises, the friends to be left behind is typically Sartrean; all is transformed by the intention to escape. The plan fails because Chalais's men had spied on them and informed the sentries. Schneider is shot and Brunet recaptured, after watching his friend die in his arms. Brunet acts finally out of friendship, realizing that party loyalty is qualified by the contradictions of opportunistic politics, and that, if there is no place in human solitude for *personal* loyalty, men are done for anyway. The fragment concludes very pessimistically, stressing the solitary human condition. In the unpublished portions, Brunet was to rehabilitate Schneider's name and act henceforth in true freedom, rather than submit to an absolute dictated by others; Mathieu, who was not killed after all, was to become a resistance fighter and die a hero; both Philippe and Boris were to end likewise. Sartre said that the first volumes of his series were "no more than an inventory of false, mutilated, incomplete freedoms" and that the fourth volume was to define what he meant by true liberty (*WS*, 115, 233–34). This is the critique of freedom, not its realization.[19] The title of the series is thus unintentionally ironic, and it is only in later works that the meaning of freedom is carried farther.

Sartre's career as a fiction writer includes noteworthy successes: *La Nausée* and *Le Sursis* are excellent novels that make versatile use of varied techniques to explore the confrontation of consciousness and the world and its implications; *Le Mur* shows equal mastery of technique and subject. In all volumes, character portrayal is expert, dialogue suits the characters, plot is well handled, and ordinary experiences of life are revealing. While some may believe his drama to be superior, the argument can be made that fiction shows off to better advantage his phenomenologist's understanding of how consciousness creates the world, enters into relationships with others, takes cognizance of its body, and is responsible for all values, because fiction allows the writer to explore both directly and symbolically the unspoken, the stream of consciousness which Husserl describes and which is conveyed through the Sartrean interior monologue and authorial omniscience. It also allows for a more highly metaphorical language, giving full value to the imagination. In spite of some tediousness, a heavy dose of ideology, and other flaws, Sartre's fiction is a successful exploration of inner and outer conflicts, for-itself and for-others—the drama of subjectivities in an objective world.

Chapter Five

The Early Drama

Introduction

Sartre's career as a dramatist, which began in the prison camp at Trèves when at Christmas 1940 he produced and acted in *Bariona,* is tied to action, or what he calls praxis, which is the essence of drama according to the Aristotelian definition.[1] Perhaps this stress on action helps explain why he continued to compose plays for ten years after abandoning fiction and wrote many provocative pages on the theater.[2] To him, the drama seemed a privileged form of expressing situations, in the sense used in *L'Etre et le néant*—man's position in the world defined by its obstacles in relation to a freely chosen end; the context in which freedom is expressed and within which projects are realized as acts (*TS,* 19–20). In fact, his whole ontology is dramatic, since it supposes not a static but a dynamic human reality, in a situation, in conflict with the in-itself, others, and itself (see *S* IX, 12). The thrust of human reality forward toward its possibilities, which is called time, is itself a dramatic action.

Sartre's talent is to translate this drama of existence into concrete, stageworthy situations, which often have a political element. His predilection for extreme, violent circumstances—the "limit situations" noted also in connection with his fiction[3]—has both a philosophic basis and an historical one. Philosophically speaking, it is the extreme situation which makes the need for choice more obvious, thus arousing greater anguish and putting man in a clearer confrontation with himself and his freedom. If to exist is to exercise the freedom he is, then human realization is most nearly complete when the problem of choice is most acute and bears the greatest consequences. Historically, Sartrean drama is rooted in the crises of the forties and fifties. He noted that the meaning of freedom was never greater than during the Occupation, when every act signified a clear political choice and often carried the possibility of arrest, imprisonment, and death, for oneself and others (*SH,* 55–57). Like Malraux, he is interested in the implications of torture (*TS,* 241). This emphasis on violence and death, which remove the play from the domain of mores and ordinary psychology and place it in the realm of ethical and existential choice, the stuff of which the greatest drama has been made, may be explained also by his wish to depart from the entrenched traditions that dominated theater in France earlier, especially its psychologism and its bourgeois orientation.[4]

He also wished to reintroduce into the French theater a stylized, almost mythic quality which it had generally lost.[5] This was from a desire to point up the crucial questions at the heart of drama more than total realism does, partly because the public is so accustomed to realism that it is blasé, and because realism falsifies the ideas of freedom and will, partly because stylization is an ingredient of the tension of drama (*TS,* 61). He borrowed one topic from Greek classical drama, translated a Greek play, and drew on other such "myths" as heaven and hell, and a range of political stereotypes that have become modern myths.[6] Nevertheless, his theater remains bourgeois, in the tradition of the well-made play, even approaching the theater of the boulevards.[7] It is almost entirely in prose, rarely of a poetic quality; with exceptions, the characters are of the middle class. Domestic and personal issues—love, sexuality, family relationships, the self—occupy the first rank frequently, and the love triangle is common. Realism is strong even in hell; Sartre's imagination remains mimetic. Political questions do enlarge the scope of his drama, but the proletariat is rarely visible, and though the choices involve life and death, they generally concern only a few destinies. In short, the plane of the universal is less visible here than in the fictional masterpieces of Malraux and Camus involving choice and struggle. In truth, the bourgeois setting suits Sartre, and his strength may be, if not psychology, the depiction of concrete relationships between human beings, not the general human situation.

Les Mouches and *Huis-clos*

Les Mouches, Sartre's first public production, contemporary with *L'Etre et le néant,* is also a reflection of the Occupation.[8] Presented in 1943 by Charles Dullin (who also acted in it), the play, a retelling in three acts of the story of Orestes' revenge, is concerned thematically (as is *Bariona*) with freedom—primarily ontological, but also political, as was patent to the first spectators. That it passed the German censors is explained variously by their stupidity and their artistic liberalism. Though not a stage success, it is considered one of Sartre's best plays. It remains moderately close to the classical sources; there is a modern parallel in the *Electre* of Giraudoux.[9] As in the legend, Orestes in disguise returns to Argos to find his sister Electra in slavery and Clytemnestra and Aegisthus on the throne. Their crime has become a public burden, as Aegisthus has succeeded in persuading the citizens that they are all guilty and that public penance and mourning alone can appease the gods. (This is a clear parallel with the theme of national guilt preached by the Vichy government.) The main plot consists in Orestes' meeting with Electra, their eventual recognition, the murder of the king and queen, persecution by the Furies (embodied in flies), and Orestes' departure. It is complicated by the presence of Jupiter, disguised at first, whose interest, like that of Aegisthus, lies in keeping the populace in penance; whether civil or divine, authority is based on fear. Orestes, on the contrary, tries to convince the citizens that their guilt is a royal hoax; as a blasphemer and a model iconoclast, he is dangerous to Jupiter. The significance of the murders lies less in revenge, as in the classical models, than in the proclamation of total human freedom. Ironically, Electra, who for fifteen years had hoped for her brother's return and the punishment of the royal couple, does not have the courage to live with the dreadful act: after Clytemnestra's murder, she adopts the guilt that characterizes her fellow citizens, leaving Orestes alone with his act, in typical existentialist solitude.

Dramatically, the high point is the confrontation between Orestes and Jupiter, in which the former declares his freedom and the latter admits that though he rules the universe, he is not ruler of men. Departing here from its sources, the play puts greater emphasis on this philosophical discovery than on the horrors of adultery and murder, and gives primacy to the individual. Until it is exercised by choice and assumption of all its consequences, liberty is nothing; it does not mean being able to change the past, but to identify with an act, that is, commitment. It is not a feature of man, it *is* man, and condemns him to live as a stranger, in exile, without excuse, and to invent his values. It has been suggested that Sartre is putting on trial here his own status as an intellectual (*SV,* 144). When Orestes first arrives, he is, though educated, without a genuine past; his is a fallow freedom. After his act, he can claim something for himself and thus create authentic being. He does this, moreover, in others' name as well as his own and thus proclaims himself as a savior; in a passage which may allude to Christ, he says he has sacrificed himself for the people who did not recognize him; but, rather than being killed, he is a killer.[10] In his last speeches, he assumes the despair which is his lot, along with his "obscene and insipid existence" (or, as the translation puts it, "foul and futile"), and tells Jupiter, in the famous phrase, that "life begins on the far side of despair." Free, he departs from Argos, followed by the Furies, leaving the citizens to rebegin.

The text abounds in Sartrean notions now familiar but perhaps puzzling in 1943: the future as visible, already present in the mode of not-being; the mode of for-others (as in Orestes' wish not to rule Argos from the throne but rather to occupy the citizens' minds); the mode of bad faith; the dead as in-itself, identical at last to themselves and turning the living also into objects because their image is forever arrested in the dead; the rights which material comfort seems to grant; the self as empty; the force of the gaze (Electra's turnabout is caused in part because she imagines her mother's face in agony). The text is not felicitous in all respects: the contrast between, on the one hand, the fabulous element, Greek heroes, and benighted Argos, and, on the other, Orestes' modern preoccupation with self-identity and freedom, not to mention the political implications, is sometimes jarring, and several long speeches are tedious, as are the scenes where the citizens make public confession and try to placate the spirits of the dead. But the Promethean strength of Orestes' stand against Jupiter is memorable and puts the play in the great Nietzschean tradition which proclaims that God is dead and man alone is responsible for himself.

Huis-clos (No Exit), probably Sartre's most famous play and a great stage success, takes its title from a judicial term meaning a closed hearing, and thus, like "Le Mur" and "La Chambre," introduces the theme of sequestration as well as that of judgment. Composed in 1944, it was originally intended for three friends of Sartre who were to act in it. Camus was later to play the role of Garcin, but relinquished it to a professional actor for the May premiere. The play's one act is a treatise on the relationships between human beings, or the for-others. Sartre later said that the famous phrase "Hell is others" did not necessarily apply to all relationships, and that freedom would allow one to break out of the circle, but at the period of *Huis-clos* and *L'Etre et le néant* the statement seems universally valid (*WS,* 98–99; *TS,* 237–40).

The action takes place in a room in hell. One by one the three who are to be each other's torturers arrive. While knowing full well why he is there, each lies to the other about his past. A necessary first step in establishing what will be their eternal relationship is confession; the way in which each is led by the others to do so is part of the dynamics of the play. Far from creating a sense of solidarity, their crimes merely separate them and enable each to persecute the others. Inès the lesbian will continually try to seduce Estelle and make her hate the only available man, Garcin. She is a sadist;

she needs, she says, the suffering of others to exist. Estelle, the most superficial, an adulteress and murderer, cares only for men and pesters Garcin, yet does not even care what his character is like and thus cannot justify him. She can torment Inès by making love to Garcin, but Inès can reciprocate by refusing to reflect to her the image she craves: for there are no mirrors in hell and the existence of each must be mediated through others. Garcin, who tries to remain aloof and meditate on the motivation for his acts, is nevertheless drawn into the relationships because of Estelle's advances and because he too needs a witness. Though his crime was mistreating his wife, he is bothered chiefly by doubts about his courage, and he wants the others to reflect to him what he wishes to believe—that his flight upon outbreak of war was an act of pacifist conviction rather than cowardice. Since Estelle, who is soft like an octopus, cannot make any such judgment, Garcin must turn to Inès, who recognizes his act as cowardice, at least insofar as, once he is dead, its value is forever fixed and nothing can follow it to redeem it; his colleagues on earth have already judged him this way. Garcin needs her favorable opinion so much that, when finally the door opens, he cannot leave.

The conflict between subject and object is shown with great skill, as each person is alternately torturer and tortured. There is no escape: in hell there are neither eyelids nor darkness to veil the gaze of others. In a way, this is orthodox: punishment is appropriate to the crime, as in Dante's inferno, and the consequences of one's acts endure. But it is meant of course not as an intimation of afterlife but as a reflection of human reality here on earth, enclosed in a pattern of search for self-affirmation through others, whether masochistically or sadistically. The only possible authenticity is in the assumption and thus reevaluation of one's choices—the contrary of guilt, as Orestes saw; and in the closed room of hell without future, death prevents the retouching of one's life; one is the sum of his acts.

Morts sans sépulture and La Putain respectueuse

Morts sans sépulture (translated as The Victors, from an earlier discarded title), presented at the Théâtre Antoine in November 1946, is considered by Sartre and others among the weakest of his plays.[11] Yet it is valuable to those interested in the dramatic rendering of his ideas. It alone among his early plays has as its setting contemporary France—in this case, German-occupied territory in 1944. Sartre composed the play as a deliberate reminder of the Resistance, when the former collaborators were reappearing (*C, 239*). It reintroduces the theme of sequestration, since it concerns members of the Resistance held captive, tortured, and put to death. In French theatrical tradition, any shocking, bloody action must be banned from the stage; Sartre's violation of these proprieties (still in effect in the 1940s, as the scandalized audiences proved) is another way of undermining bourgeois values, though he denied this motive, and creating a very different theater.

Whereas many Sartrean works present notably unheroic figures, there are suggestions here in both political and philosophic terms of heroism, made possible in part by the existence of clear-cut evil, embodied in the militia, the tool of the Germans. But there is no *single* form of good or heroism to counterbalance evil, but rather a range of possibilities, some involving only oneself, others relationships with fellow captives, so that choice is necessary and difficult. The play centers around conduct under torture. Before the questioning, each captive is preoccupied with how he will react. Lucie calls upon love to strengthen her, Canoris upon the memory of previous torture he had successfully endured; François, Lucie's young brother, is totally without courage. Henri, perhaps the most interesting character, wants to identify the cause of his strong sense of guilt and have a reason for suffering, to give some meaning to his action and death. Sorbier tries to imagine the scene beforehand because his sense of self is bound up with how he will behave. François tries to dissociate himself from the others and their acts of sabotage, claiming that he is innocent—contrary to the Sartrean precept of responsibility for all. Since they believe they will not survive, the captives are already as if dead, and their projects have become senseless.

The dynamics of the group change when, after Henri is tortured and as Sorbier is being interrogated elsewhere, the Resistance leader Jean, whose whereabouts the militia wish to learn, is brought in by the guards. They have not yet identified him and are checking his alibi. Now that the prisoners have an important secret to keep, their behavior can have practical consequences. It becomes clear, however, that if they refuse to speak, it will be not to save Jean but to win out over their tormentors: the subject-object relationship is such that, even under torture, their accusing gaze can dominate their captors if they do not give in. Sorbier is terribly ashamed because he cried out. Moreover, because he is not to be tortured, Jean becomes an outsider; he does not share in the humiliation which creates bonds that go beyond politics and even the love between him and

Lucie. Lucie observes that she and her tormentors now form a couple—
since her objectification in shame, and her defiance of them, create the
basic for-others relationship.

When all (except Sorbier, who has managed to jump from a window,
killing himself) realize that François will break when his turn comes,
Henri strangles him, with Lucie's tacit permission. Perhaps, as Jean says,
this is from pride: Henri and the others do not want their moral victory to
be snatched from them.[12] They all claim responsibility for the act.
Meanwhile, Jean, who is to be set free, tells them to reveal a false location
for him, thus avoiding further torture. When one of the militiamen
proposes to let the group go free if they reveal the information, the
practical Canoris urges the others to agree. Only by living will they give
the true meaning of patriotism, rather than pride, to their resistance.
Lucie and Henri first refuse; their killing of François is justifiable only if
they too die, and Henri is concerned with "saving" his death by having it
consistent with what preceded. But when she hears fresh rain and imagines
the smell of wet earth, Lucie consents. Ironically, the agreement is not
honored: they are shot anyway. Thus everything is taken from them: their
resistance under torture loses its meaning when they give in, and their
final embrace of life ends in death. Though less well motivated, the ending
is not unlike that of "Le Mur."

One of the most Sartrean aspects of the play is the idea of total
responsibility. The resistants, who were supposed to take a village, failed
because it was practically impossible; yet they are at fault anyway. Even
under torture, one is free and thus responsible; there is no excuse for
yielding, whence the anguish beforehand and sense of shame afterward.
Another Sartrean element is the ambiguity of action—in its motivation
and consequences. In the absence of set values to which one has merely to
subscribe, choices have to be made in context, with risks for oneself and
others, and there is no purity possible. One notes also the uselessness of
life, which seems meaningless and unjustified unless it is connected to a
collective project. The world will be just as full after their death as now,
says Henri. Lucie's turnabout at the end is unwarranted philosophically,
since nothing in her has survived the torture, her love neither of country,
Jean, nor brother, and life is futile anyway—though perhaps it is to be
expected psychologically and echoes many other denouements where, after
death and destruction, order again prevails and hope is possible. Solitude
and futility are the final marks of the characters' lives and deaths; they
cannot offer true fraternity to each other and are, like the torturers, at most
witnesses to the others' humiliation. The political meaning of their action

does not endure any more than the personal meaning. The "unburied dead" of the title are they—cut off from everyone—and their useless projects, claimed by no one. Ultimately, heroism is impossible even if one does not cry out under torture, since it undermines itself by its ambiguous, contradictory origin and results; aspiring to be, it is a useless passion.

La Putain respectueuse (The Respectful Prostitute), presented at the Théâtre Antoine in November 1946, which introduced into French the euphemism "la respectueuse," is one of Sartre's weakest works, melodramatic and built around stereotypes, with inaccuracies which bother the American reader. Because of the title and what some took to be its anti-Americanism, it caused repeated scandals.[13] A New York woman, Lizzie, a version of the "prostitute with a heart of gold," moving south, witnesses in the train an unjustified shooting of a black man by a white from a good family, a "leader." Both a young man, Fred, and his father, a senator, attempt to get her to testify that the Negro tried to rape her and attacked the whites first. Fred frames her and attempts to blackmail her, but she is willing to go to jail rather than bear false witness. The senator is more subtle: he persuades her by appealing to her pity for the attacker's mother and in the name of public utility, since the white man is a solid, useful citizen. Taken in by his rhetoric, she signs the false statement, although she feels she has been duped. The Negro, somewhat implausibly, twice tries to hide at her apartment from a lynch mob. Finally she gives him a pistol so that he may defend himself, but he cannot shoot a white. Fred fires at him despite her protests; she then tries to shoot Fred but like the black cannot fire at a member of a dominant caste. When Fred offers to make her his mistress, she yields to her sexual desire for him.

However cliché-riddled the play may be, one cannot deny validity in its criticism of a two-standard society, divided along racial and class lines, its accusations of American sexual hypocrisy, and the particularly Sartrean attack on proper people who take themselves as an absolute and assume rights over others, causing them to exist in shame. It suggests that the sources of racial and sexual prejudice are not only in biological, economic, and social factors, but in the fundamental bad faith which marks most human projects.

Les Mains sales

In Sartre's 1948 play *Les Mains sales (Dirty Hands)*,[14] human and ideological dynamics meet in an action involving matters as diverse as the self and its motivation, marriage, political principle versus expediency, the education of women, and class hostility. It is a murder mystery where the question is not who shot the victim but why he was shot and what it means to be the author of an act. With echoes of *Hamlet, Le Cid,* and Musset's *Lorenzaccio* (*WS,* 193), and very imaginative language, it is literary, but gives to age-old psychological problems of intention and action a new form. The work was a success in its initial staging at the Théâtre Antoine and was produced in several foreign countries. The film version, with Pierre Brasseur as Hoederer, is excellent.[15]

Unlike Sartre's previous plays, it does not follow the unities of place, time, and action. It consists of a flashback in five tableaux inserted between two others, the first furnishing the exposition of the problem, the last the solution, while the middle tableaux explore its development, as Hugo recounts to his fellow Communist Olga the events leading to Hoederer's death. On the chief plot questions—the reason that Hugo murdered Hoederer and his current usefulness to the party—the final outcome will turn. But within the flashback the question is rather whether Hugo will be able to kill Hoederer, a socialist leader in a central European country (perhaps modeled on Hungary, with certain resemblances to France) during World War II, who is to be liquidated because he is too willing to compromise with bourgeois and Fascist elements for political expediency.

Hugo is an educated youth of the upper bourgeoisie who joined the party in protest over social inequality. The flashback first shows him begging party leaders to assign him the task of assassinating Hoederer so that he can prove himself and justify his existence. Like Sorbier, he wants to put himself to the test. While still clinging to certain bourgeois values, he is intransigent, obsessed with discipline, given to absolutes, and preoccupied with himself. Although he wishes to deny his family and says he has joined the party to forget himself, he carries around photos of himself as a boy. All his behavior has a personal aspect as well as a political one. Hoederer's proletarian bodyguards, who resent him, are right in seeing him as an intellectual and an individualist, facing problems quite different from theirs.

When he is sent with his wife, Jessica, to act as Hoederer's secretary, in a situation of semisequestration, they are both impressed by him. Their own superficial relationship, based on role-playing and the mediation of the other, seems very flimsy compared to the solid, virile force of Hoederer. As a woman, whose justification traditionally depends on men's recognition, Jessica is particularly susceptible. Hugo subsequently has ample opportunity to shoot Hoederer, but finds himself unable to. Like Hamlet, he examines his conscience, in which resolution and irresolution war, for reasons he cannot understand but which Jessica identifies as Hoederer's influence on him. He even questions his own reality insofar as he is merely unrealized potentiality. When Hoederer and Hugo, who is drunk, quarrel, he becomes angry enough to seize his pistol; but at that very moment, Olga, fearing the consequences of his procrastination, steals the opportunity from him by hurling a bomb herself. Hugo later argues with Jessica, who persuades him to present his objections to Hoederer and listen to *his* point of view. Hoederer presents plainly the arguments for a *Realpolitik* suitable to his party's interests in the current circumstances and argues that one cannot govern without dirtying one's hands. The real criterion is efficacity, not principle. He accepts the necessity of an imperfect good and consents to the sole responsibility for his choices. In spite of his ascendency over him, Hugo still insists to Jessica that the leader is objectively a traitor. The next day, informed by Jessica and suspecting Hugo's intentions anyway, Hoederer convinces him to give up his pistol and invites him to work *with* him instead of against him. Ironically, as Hugo returns to accept the offer, Hoederer, seduced by Jessica, is kissing her; Hugo shoots, not so much from sexual jealousy (their love is false anyway) as from the supposition that Hoederer had offered his friendship only through interest in Jessica.

The crime, therefore, is ambiguous. It depends on chance and an ironic misunderstanding, and on Jessica's behavior, based on her fascination for real men and real ideas mixed with inability to take things seriously. It is closest to being an act of wounded ego and thus individualistic in the extreme. Hugo does not deceive himself that it is a political murder, but now believes it should have been one, since his reflections in prison have convinced him again that Hoederer was objectively wrong, however sincere his convictions. When Olga questions him, he is still unable to determine the true motives for his act. Was it the order from the party? "The orders? There was no order, not any more. The order stayed behind and I went on alone and killed alone," he observes, stressing the anguish and solitude of all decisions.[16] Yet the act is alienated from him, and he is obsessed with uniting its objectivity with his own empty subjectivity, which disappears as soon as he looks at it. Trying to assess it, Olga is pleased to see that the act remains separate from him. She wants him to forget it, since the party has now changed its tactics and is following the very policy of Hoederer. This revelation brings about the denouement. To have the act's best meaning taken from him is to deny to it, and thus himself, all meaning. With his cry that he is not salvageable, he finally claims the killing fully as his own. At the same time, he gives meaning to Hoederer's death, making it a death for his ideas, not a stupid crime of passion.

Nowhere in Sartre's imaginative work is there a better illustration of the absence of an ego within consciousness and of human essence. Hugo constantly feels that he is not quite real; he is empty, a meaningless potentiality, a subjectivity opposed to others' objectivity. Like the characters in *Huis-clos,* he appeals to others to give him a sense of self and aspires to the solidity he supposes them to have. But their mediation is insufficient, particularly that of Jessica, who refuses to see him as truly committed. His narcissism is an attempt to apprehend himself as genuine. Since man is what he does, only an act can give him his identity by committing this freedom. Although the murder is carried out almost despite him, for motives not political, he can assume responsibility for it retrospectively, and then his existence will have a significance, which is his self.

Politically, the play was not intended as an indictment of Communist orthodoxy or methods, though anti-Soviet and Communist authorities (very hostile) alike interpreted it as such. It is rather an exploration of certain difficulties of Communism in the late 1940s, especially that of young bourgeois intellectuals who turned to the party but found that they could neither entirely deny their class nor be wholly accepted.[17] It confronts also the Sartrean issue of praxis—how to act in a world of time, where there are no absolutes. It illustrates what he calls elsewhere the conflict between right and right (*TS,* 60, 136–37). "I justify everyone," he said of the work (*WS,* 187). He gives his preference, however, to opportunism: dramatically speaking, Hoederer is stronger than Hugo; his arguments are supported by the maturity and strength of character, or solidity, which Hugo lacks. Moreover, his opponents do not disagree with him on principle, really, but on tactics—they think the alliance with other parties ill-timed—so that Hugo is alone in refusing to make political concessions. This is because he has transferred to Communism his middle-class idealism. Sartre stated that Hugo was not modeled on him and that, if he were a revolutionary, he would prefer to be like Hoederer. Ultimately, the text depicts political as well as philosophic ambiguity— the tension which characterizes all choice.

Films

Sartre's first ventures in filmmaking were contemporary with his beginnings as a playwright, and his view of the cinema as an art form remained essentially theatrical.[18] His first efforts, scripts written for Pathé during the Occupation, included, with some never produced, *Les Jeux sont faits (The Chips Are Down)*, screened and published in 1947. *L'Engrenage (In the Mesh)* was published in 1948 and produced as a play but never as a film. Both scripts, while interesting, are inferior in their written form to his plays and fiction.

The earlier one is often taken as an illustration of bad faith.[19] Pierre and Eve are allowed to return from the dead for twenty-four hours and will be granted a full lifetime if they can prove that they love each other completely. It is as if the characters in *Huis-clos* were permitted to return to earth for a day. Each has other concerns—Eve, her sister, and Pierre, the imminent insurrection of which he was the organizer—to which he also feels committed. Toward the deadline, Pierre finds himself obliged to remain with his fellow revolutionaries, who are about to die as their revolt is crushed—although they have turned against him because of his strange and compromising behavior. He says Eve could not love him, nor he respect himself, if he did not try to save them. This Cornelian solution to the love-duty dilemma is interpreted by the otherworldly authorities as a failure to love. Readers have supposed that it is the fault of Pierre and Eve and that, refusing to recognize their freedom, they are in bad faith when they say the chips were already down. Sartre specified, however, that the story was not existentialist but rather determinist (*WS*, 163). It is built on the notion of authority: love must measure up to given standards, and is more an entity than a mode of living, whereas according to existentialist views man creates his love in a situation, not to satisfy some external criteria. Yet the film is one of the rare Sartrean works where love does seem possible, where the other is no longer a threat, and where a creative relationship can be an authentic project. It is ironic that the denouement should condemn it. One could argue for the film's ethical superiority despite aesthetic inferiority.

The background of revolution in *Les Jeux sont faits* becomes the foreground in *L'Engrenage* (originally called "Les Mains sales"), the story of two similar uprisings in a small country resembling certain Latin-American nations.[20] The title refers to the gearwork of historical necessity in which successful revolutionaries are caught, especially the need to sacrifice the innocent. Built on the classic conflict between principle and expediency, revolutionary idealism and organizational necessity, the film consists of courtroom scenes and flashbacks, where witnesses recount various moments in the life of a dictator, now on trial before a popular tribunal. Several episodes are presented thrice, from varying points of

view; the characters change dress and appearance according to who the
narrator is. Thus Sartre suggests visually the perspectival quality of reality,
created by intentions. Jean Aguerra, who came to power in an earlier
revolution, is accused of treason. He refuses to defend himself until the
name of Hélène, the woman he loved, is sullied; then he, like her and
others, tells his version of the past. Having sacrificed to practical aims his
close friend Lucien, as well as his principles, he argues for his policies
much as Hoederer does, and refuses to disown his acts: even if the event
proves him wrong, his choice was made in the best interests of the
revolution as he then saw it. His death sentence confirms the ambiguity of
action. Yet his right is not the only one; he admits that idealists are needed
too. At the conclusion, the new revolutionary ruler meets with envoys of a
foreign power, who assure him they will invade if nationalization of the
petroleum industry is declared. Reluctantly, like Aguerra before him, he
promises not to carry out the platform of appropriation on which his group
came to power; he too is caught in the gears of power politics, and the
circle is complete.

Sartre contributed scripts for a number of other films, including several
based on his own works, and a version of Arthur Miller's *The Crucible*.
Only fragments of these have been published. His interest in the cinema
was enduring, but his contributions to it inferior to those in other genres,
perhaps because his work is extremely verbal, and also because his
viewpoints on man and his situation require a subtlety of expression that
scenarios rarely give. Despite their merits, in particular, the very interesting study of revolution in *L'Engrenage*, his scripts are simplistic next to
other texts.

Chapter Six
The Later Drama
Introduction

Sartre's three later plays and two adaptations, composed between 1951 and 1965, mirror and to some extent spring from the significant changes in his thinking provoked by postwar politics, the Cold War, and his consequent move toward Marxism. Though they are not all mainly political, all have political aspects, which reveal how his dislike of the bourgeoisie had become a fully rationalized position, grounded in Marxism. In different ways, all are very theatrical, and generally more complex than the early ones. Their approach to philosophical and social problems is somewhat more nuanced; the situations go beyond questions of individual freedom, to the plane of history and its dialectic.

The later plays are also thematically alike. Three themes which inform *Les Mots* and the study on Genet are illustrated brilliantly here. The first is bastardy. Though Sartre was legitimate, his father's early death and his consequent upbringing by his mother and grandparents gave him the sense of being fatherless, a circumstance which he viewed as an advantage, since the basic paternal role is to exercise authority over the child's freedom. This attitude recalls Gide's view that the bastard, freed from the obligation to fulfill an image and carry on a family destiny, is able to invent his values; he alone is authentic. Sartre puts greater stress on a kind of schizophrenia induced within the illegitimate child by the fact that to others he is flawed by birth, whereas, like everyone else, to himself he is an absolute, perfect freedom. The other thus becomes internalized, and the theme of illegitimacy, first illustrated in *Le Diable et le Bon Dieu,* joins in *Kean* that of playacting, since the bastard does not quite know which self is real.[1] He thus feels characteristically untrue to himself. This introduces the theme of treachery, a second recurring one in the later theater, and one which is very close to Sartre's own apprehension of himself.[2] Sartre had betrayed his class by his intellectual and political positions, just as, metaphorically speaking, he was a "bastard" by virtue of his self-willed radical separation from his childhood and milieu. As for imposture or role-playing, the third major theme, it springs from the effort to be as the in-itself, as *L'Etre et le néant* showed. While it is a basic form of bad faith, shared by everyone, it is especially marked in cases where the person consciously acts a role, as with the actor and the impostor. This theme also has Gidean overtones, echoing his meditations on sincerity and the self. It reflects Sartre's own experiments with playacting when, as a child, he assigned himself roles in extremely romanesque adventures, and came to feel that his very existence was a simulacrum. Already present in *Les Mains sales,* where Hugo is neither wholly a secretary nor wholly an assassin, and an important element of Sartre's analysis of Genet, the theme is splendidly illustrated in *Kean* and *Nekrassov.*

Le Diable et le Bon Dieu

This play in three acts, Sartre's favorite (*C,* 242), composed in 1951 and produced that year by Louis Jouvet (with Pierre Brasseur as the hero and Jean Vilar as Heinrich), is one of Sartre's most provocative, and a major statement on ethics.[3] Long and cumbersome, requiring a vast cast and elaborate staging, it has a Shakespearean mixture of seriousness and humor, loftiness and crudity, individual and collective drama; it seems both historical and very modern. It adheres to neither the unity of place nor of time. Among modern authors, its breadth and ambition can be compared best to those of Claudelian drama.[4] It bears some resemblance to Romantic theater, although with Goethe's *Goetz von Berlichingen* it shares only the hero's name (see *C,* 166). The original inspiration came from a play by Cervantes, *El Rufián dichoso,* about which Jean-Louis Barrault had told Sartre in 1943; he also borrowed features of medieval mysteries. The play deals with the powerful Promethean and Faustian ambitions which characterize the Renaissance and Romanticism.[5] It is also a social docu-ment, focusing on class struggle in Reformation Germany (with obvious resemblances with contemporary proletarian struggle). The hero, Goetz, is a bastard, born of a peasant and a noblewoman, whose situation as an outcast has led him not only to pursue ordinary success—already attained as a military leader—but also to strive toward a superior plane of being, by means of evil, since it is more inventive than good (already done by God), and since he alone can be responsible for it; only hatred and weakness are entirely human. He thus opposes himself to God, his only worthy adversary. His political position is anarchism; he is cut off from the masses, among whom social change arises.

Goetz has betrayed his legitimate brother Conrad, with whom he had formed an alliance, and has thus given victory to the archbishop. He nonetheless has laid siege to the city of Worms, source of the archbishop's revenues, and is going to starve it mercilessly. Within Worms, Heinrich, a priest, who is the antagonist, is torn between loyalty to the ordinary folk and loyalty to the church, in the person of its bishop and priests, all imprisoned by the rebellious citizens. He watches as the people assassinate the bishop, who, dying, gives him a key to a passage below the city walls. He can use it to save the lives either of the imprisoned priests or the vaster numbers of Worms citizens. Heinrich, not Goetz, is the most treacherous character of the play. He takes the key to Goetz in his camp outside of Worms and struggles between the temptation to give it away so that the army can enter immediately and free the priests, while massacring the populace, and reluctance to betray the people, from whom he came. The scenes between Heinrich and Goetz suggest the complexity of human motivation. The priest confesses that he hates the poor, whom he claims to love; yet he says he will not sacrifice them, although he ultimately hands over the key. His character is weak or, in Sartrean terms, he chooses treason because he prefers it. Goetz resolves to massacre the populace that very night, though a banker would pay him handsomely to spare it; he prefers destruction to profit. When Nasty, a peasant leader who attacks the Catholic hierarchy, claims divine inspiration, and tries to prepare for an eventual popular uprising against authority, proposes that Goetz join him in a campaign to drive out the church and princes, he refuses; he would rather make God suffer through his violence. He tells God that if He wishes it not to happen, He can send a sign; but the heavens are silent.

Heinrich reasons with Goetz that his evil is unimpressive, since anyone can do it; furthermore, evil is *all* man can do: good is impossible. Thus challenged, Goetz wants to wager that henceforth he will do only good. But, Heinrich observes, to do good in order to win a bet cancels the good. Goetz proposes to let a roll of the dice decide his conduct, leaving the responsibility with God. If he rolls higher, he will continue to do evil. His mistress Catherine later reveals that he cheated, rolling the lower number in order to make his *own* choice and show up God. Thus converted to good, he agrees to safe passage for the priests of Worms and ends the siege. He also pardons those who were to be tortured and sends Catherine away. In a year and a day Heinrich is to return to judge Goetz's success. The undertaking is clearly Faustian, a fact which is underscored when Heinrich is accompanied later by an invisible devil.

Nasty embodies the two most powerful social forces in sixteenth-century Germany, peasant revolt and Protestantism. His position, that of the pragmatic militant, is entirely objective. For instance, he tells the people that the bishop is responsible for their hunger, since he is the head of a wealthy church, and calls Heinrich a traitor because, as a peasant, he has joined forces with the established church. He argues that the seizure of aristocrats' lands is premature, whereas Goetz wants the people's cause to triumph immediately. "Good has to be served like a soldier," says Nasty, but Goetz proudly wants to create it singlehandedly.[6] His efforts to do good take the radical form of giving to the peasants the lands he had acquired after Conrad's defeat and death, and of establishing a utopia, "The City of the Sun." Catherine, literally dying of love for him, fears damnation because of her sins. When she sees horrible visions of devils, the people avoid her, but Goetz comforts her by saying he will take her sins upon himself. As a sign, he asks that God send him stigmata. When they do not appear, he stabs himself and shows Catherine the wounds. After her death he confronts Hilda, who has renounced her wealth to be with the people and who accuses God of His indifference to human suffering. Since she perceives that he helps the peasants from pride, not from love, she is hostile. Giving, Sartre points out, is humiliating: far from creating equality, it draws attention to the freedom of the giver to give but not the receiver to refuse. Goetz has practiced charity, an essentially conservative position. Meanwhile, his example of giving away his lands has incited hundreds of other peasants to attempt, unsuccessfully, to seize their lords' estates. Although Goetz's followers adhere to a doctrine of nonviolence, they are massacred: neither peasant rebels nor barons can tolerate their passive neutrality.[7] With Heinrich's help, Nasty tries to forestall the revolt, which he deems premature, but fails. He then begs Goetz to prevent total massacre by taking command of the army and forcing the barons to sue for peace, but Goetz refuses, urged by Hilda, who loves him. Although he returns her affection, he refuses the contamination of love, echoing medieval doctrines on the filth of the body, and rather tries to punish himself for causing his peasants' death.

When, after a year, Heinrich returns to judge him, Goetz, supported by Hilda, who ultimately prefers human to divine love, meets him willingly and admits his failure. The peasants do not love him; brotherly love is a joke, and his generosity did more harm than all his previous evil. He wants Heinrich to judge him, for others' mediation is required for the self to see the self. His reflections lead him to a conclusion which many readers have taken to be the essence of the play: that, if to do good is impossible, neither God nor the Devil exists; there is only man. Heaven is silent and the desire to do good (the dice roll) came only from himself. As Nietzsche said, man is the solution. Goetz had wanted to *be* in God's eyes; but he alone can decide and absolve himself. "God is the loneliness of man" (141). Sartre's aim was not so much to proclaim atheism—he had achieved it years before and felt no need to belabor the point—as to assert that from an atheistic position one must draw the conclusion of full human responsibility. The absolutes of good and evil, of which God alone could be the guarantor, must be replaced by relativistic ethics, based on situations; praxis must succeed morality (*WS*, 249–52). As long as Goetz pursued absolutes, he was working against human history; both the evil and good he did had bloody consequences which merely fortified oppressive institutions. As Nasty says, disorder is the best servant of established power (53). Only by seeing that history is contradictory and ambiguous, never pure, can Goetz effectively do something for men. Unlike Orestes, who leaves Argos after proclaiming human freedom, Goetz consents at last to take command of the peasant army moving against the barons, which has already been routed once and, without leadership, will be destroyed. When his authority is challenged, he strangles the challenger, thus restoring hierarchy and discipline, which are necessary for effective action. The end justifies the means; the innocent must perish for the greater good of social change.[8]

Although such a conclusion is not entirely new for Sartre, it underscores his developing concern with practical action in the context of history, viewed from the Marxist standpoint as the product of social forces progressing dialectically in a series of syntheses. Like that of Canoris in *Morts sans sépulture*, Goetz's final attitude is entirely practical; he is no longer interested in evil and will do merely what must be done for a particular end. A kind of sequel to Hugo in *Les Mains sales*, Goetz represented, Sartre said, his own transcending of the intimate contradiction he had felt from the mid-1940s on, between his belief in ontological freedom and the realization that freedom was conditioned, that men were not always able to obtain their liberty or transcend their circumstances. That is, Goetz moves from thought to action; he is "the perfect embodiment of the man of action as Sartre conceived him" (*FC*, 242–43).

If *Le Diable et le Bon Dieu* is a strong statement of atheism, outrageous to many viewers, it is more significant as an exploration of the question of ethics, in an historical and philosophic context: not what man can do to rival God, but what he must do to invent his own life and allow historical forces to be realized. Its atheism notwithstanding, its conclusion is more classical than romantic: it is concerned with earth rather than heaven, with man as he is, not as he should be. But en route to this conclusion, there are highly suggestive debates, with brilliant antitheses, on the ambiguous nature of good and evil, their inextricable entanglement, and the existence of evil under God.

Kean

Sartre's *Kean* (1953) is an adaptation in five acts of *Kean, ou Désordre et génie (Kean),* written by Alexandre Dumas the elder based on a text composed by Frédéric de Courcy and Théaulon de Saint Lambert for Frédérick Lemaître, the renowned French actor, who had met the actor Edmund Kean and, after the latter's death, wanted to play him on the stage.[9] Thus it is at several removes from the biographical reality it would purport to portray; Sartre's Kean is, as he termed him, a myth, the "patron saint of actors" (*WS,* 289), reflecting the author's interest in self-mythification. Pierre Brasseur suggested that Sartre do the adaptation; it was a great stage success. Sartre considered the subject timeless because it dealt with self-identity and allowed a great actor of each generation to test himself. His modifications are considerable. They include a tightening of the plot by reducing the cast and subplots, increased banter, greater concentration on the two heroines and an entirely different characterization of Anna, and a new interpretation of Kean's dilemmas.[10] The text bears Sartre's stamp in many ways, dealing among other topics with role-playing, bastardy, treachery, and society. It abounds in melodramatic situations and, to Sartre himself, bore some resemblance to Hugo's *Hernani,* which he liked. Sparkling with cleverness and insight, it shows how its author, sometimes heavy-handed elsewhere, could rival Giraudoux and Anouilh in Gallic wit, as in the maxim, "There's no one in the world more punctual than a woman one does not love."[11]

The play is built around four overlapping amorous triangles, which reflect on each other: Kean, the great actor, admired but socially scorned for his illegitimate birth, the Danish ambassador, and Eléna, his wife; Kean, Eléna, and the Prince of Wales, who, as his companion in pleasure, has also been his rival and chooses clothes and women because Kean likes them (a peculiar sexual form of the other as mediator to the self, or the dependence of the for-itself for its reality on the for-others); Kean, Eléna, and Anna Damby, a merchant's daughter, who wants to become both an actress and Kean's wife; and Kean, Anna, and Lord Mewill, her fiancé, who is furious that Anna should have jilted him. The dynamics of their multiple relationships cannot be conveyed by summary, nor can the probings into masculine and feminine ways of loving and the nuances of class relationships, as Sartre saw them, in early nineteenth-century England. They are indicated, however, by Kean's suggestive remark, of both social and ontological import, that he, the prince, and Anna are alike: he was born too low, the prince too high, and Anna a woman. Alienated from the dominant society, none can easily achieve authenticity.

Within this social context, Sartre explores the ambiguous relationships between actor and role, and between man and actor. These aspects of the more general relationship between self and self and the distance between subjective and objective images introduce the major Sartrean theme of imposture, which he had already considered at length as the phenomenological problem of appearances versus reality. It can be expressed as a question of the identity of the self, one of the most characteristic of modern themes.[12] Who is Kean? To most of London, he is Hamlet, Romeo, or Othello; that is why Eléna and Anna are attracted to him. He is also, socially speaking, an outcast, because he is a bastard as well as an actor. Both views are condescending; they are in the Romantic tradition that makes the audience at once applaud and scorn the buffoon, while misunderstanding his genius. To the prince, he is a charming companion; the former is not unaware that Kean takes pleasure in spiting the aristocrats by seducing their wives as well as by dominating them with his talent. To Kean himself, he is a project, felt and lived from the inside, carrying with him the past of his humble beginnings, which he validates in a sense by his success but which he feels in some way to have betrayed. He is also, for himself, the roles he has played and a pariah, since others see him thus; the for-itself and the for-others are again in conflict. He even reaches the point of "acting himself" and views himself as a man who thinks he is an actor who thinks he is Hamlet who thinks he is Fortinbras—just a series of reflections and impostures. When he tries to live for himself and be simply Kean, it is impossible: Eléna is in love with the tragedian and accepts his suit only if it is expressed dramatically, the prince finds him amusing only because he is an actor, and Lord Mewill can applaud him but never fight him in a duel. In short, Kean the impostor cannot locate his true self.

The fourth act is built around a play within a play. At Brasseur's request, Sartre replaced the scene of *Romeo and Juliet* in the Dumas text with the final scenes of *Othello*.[13] They have the advantage of making Kean attempt to reproduce on the stage the emotions he is truly feeling. His real jealousy (since the prince too is courting Eléna) prohibits him from playing Othello successfully. Sartre's interpretation recalls Diderot's thesis that a player is more effective if he is emotionally removed from his role. Provoked by Eléna's flirtations with the prince, he ruins his career by interrupting the scene and addressing directly first the prince, then her and the other spectators. He explores his existence as a self (perhaps nonexistent) within an actor (public image) within a role (stage image) and concludes that he does not exist at all. But this is the spectators' fault: as he says, they have taken a man and made of him a monster, with no reality, destined only to entertain them by playacting and thus to veil from them their own emptiness and their own imposture (which consists in part of their empty hereditary privileges). In the fifth act, he forswears his acting and looks forward, he says, to imprisonment (for having insulted the prince), for if one is put in prison, he must be *real*. However, his sentence is changed to exile and Anna Damby, whom Sartre called the only authentic character of the play (*WS, 291*), takes him away to New York, where it is suggested they will both act—in a more genuine society, built on work rather than hereditary privilege. This ending—which has been criticized[14]—does not solve all the problems associated with the divided self; but it points to the relationship between social structures and achieved freedom. When Anna lies to the prince so that he may continue to find Eléna interesting, illusion resumes its proper place in a society built on illusion; Kean and Anna have no need of lies.[15]

Nekrassov

Sartre's 1955 farce in eight scenes about imposture, politics, and the press, *Nekrassov,* was one of the least successful of his plays on stage and, understandably, was not well received by the newspapermen whom it attacked, in some cases by name.[16] Of the later plays, it reveals Sartre the least, and while doubtless entertaining when staged, least rewards reread-ing. Though humorous, it does not have the finer nuances of *Kean.* The portraits of the newspaper staff are caricatures; its satiric presentation of Cold War politics seems strained and dated. One of its best features is the nearly choreographic movements of pursued and pursuers.

As often in Sartre's theater, beginning with Orestes, who does not reveal his identity, the play involves an impostor. Georges de Valéra, an infamous swindler, persuades Sibilot, a journalist in whose house he hides, to save the one's skin and the other's career by passing him off as a defected

Communist, Nekrassov. This trick plays into the virulent anti-Soviet stand on which Sibilot's paper has been surviving, and circulation rises. Valéra plays his role with panache. Véronique, Sibilot's daughter, herself a left-wing journalist, reproaches him for driving the poor to despair with his invented reports on workers' misery in the Soviet Union. Though she knows his identity, she does not denounce him but rather appeals to his moral sense to save two fellow journalists who will be accused falsely of treason if their supposed association with Nekrassov is not disproven. The high point of the farce comes in scene six, where Valéra is surrounded by doting admirers, as well as Demidoff, a former Russian anxious to see whether Nekrassov is an impostor, Inspector Goblet, who wants to arrest the crook Valéra, and government strongmen, who want to prevent any harm coming to the famous defector. By promising allegiance to his one-man political party, Valéra persuades Demidoff not to expose him. He asks the editor to reinstate staff members fired on his account and to publish a denial that he is acquainted with the two accused journalists. Gradually he comes to realize that *he* is being duped; he is caught in the infernal machine of his lie, and he refuses to testify against them, even when the government guards reveal they are aware of his imposture and can expose him. Taking advantage of the general confusion, he escapes and returns to Sibilot's where again, in a very comic scene, he escapes from both Goblet and the government guards, but this time, with Véronique: for his political consciousness has been aroused. At the newspaper, Sibilot has become editor, and the play ends as he repeats exactly the words of his predecessor.

Politically, the play attacks the right-wing dominance of the French press in the early 1950s, its rabid anti-Communist propaganda, the fear of Moscow, and public paranoia about conspiracies. It also attacks economic inequalities, which make such a right-wing press possible. As Valéra says, he respects private property: as a swindler, he lives on it.[17] The farce points to willingness to violate law and morality in the name of public good, makes fun of authority, and suggests that professional ethics are totally lacking. Philosophically, it turns, like *Kean,* around the question of identity. But Valéra's assumption of Nekrassov's role is always self-conscious; he does not feel Kean's lack of identity and rather enjoys mystifying everyone. In another illustration of the theme, when someone proves to Mouton, an editorial board member, that despite his passionate anti-Communism, he is *objectively* a Communist (since he is not on a secret Soviet hit list and thus is not considered by them an enemy), his doubts about his own reality lead him to an attempt on Valéra's life. Sibilot also illustrates the theme: Valéra shows him that few people know him as Sibilot, whereas thousands take Valéra to be Nekrassov; thus the latter's identity is more genuine.

The play's conclusion is double, with the newspaper returning to normal but Valéra changing. His turnabout, of which Véronique is the agent, has been considered somewhat implausible, and the play is too patently the vehicle of Sartre's message, although as perceptive a reader as Roland Barthes admired its political criticism.[18] But the bittersweet mixture of burlesque comedy and cutting criticism of social institutions is appealing, and despite its exaggeration, the comedy achieves some of the *grinçant* quality of Anouilh's theater.

Les Séquestrés d'Altona

First presented in 1959, *Les Séquestrés d'Altona* was conceived initially, Sartre stated, as a protest against the use of torture in Algeria by French forces.[19] It thus originated as committed literature. The author had, however, lost some of his confidence in the power of drama to act on the public.[20] Moreover, in the political climate in France in 1957–59, he had so little confidence in the tolerance of the government that he did not treat the Algerian question outright, but rather chose as a setting postwar Germany and, as a specific topic, the wartime murder of a Jew and torture of prisoners. The play is thus most evidently an indictment of acts and attitudes connected with Germany's drive to power. Sartre wished its implication to be much larger, however, to apply not only to Gaullist France but to all the capitalist West, responsible for violence and imperialist wars, and, ultimately, to the whole twentieth century.[21] It reflects the dialectical views of history in the *Critique de la raison dialectique*, much as *Huis-clos* reflects Sartre's ontology of the 1940s.

Sartre stated in 1960 that drama and the stage had been dominated for 150 years by a ruling class that wished to see its own image reflected favorably—because it could not succeed otherwise in being an object for itself (thus real) and yet wished also for its own subjectivity to be represented.[22] He argued against this ideological tyranny and proposed a drama, modeled partly on Bertolt Brecht's, that would deny traditional participation of the audience (the key to bourgeois theater) and replace middle-class passion with true acts, which are the essence of character. *Les Séquestrés* is in part an attempt to realize these aims, and though the starting point is a bourgeois family (albeit the very highest bourgeoisie), he did not wish the play to propose solutions *within* this framework but rather to show something about the source of the problem and criticize the bourgeoisie itself, in its very foundation, not just individual members.[23]

As the title indicates, a major theme in the play is sequestration. Recurrent in French literature, especially as prison imagery,[24] visible in numerous Sartrean works, and related to Gide's text *La Séquestrée de Poitiers* (The Poitiers prisoner), it seems to haunt Sartre particularly.[25] In this case there are both literal sequestration—the hero's willful hiding upstairs for thirteen years—and the moral imprisonment of all the characters, as well as the vaster imprisonment wrought by modern history. The purely psychological dimension—which seems to dominate in scenes of the hero's pathological ravings—is less important than the ideological.

The time of the action is after the war, with flashbacks indicated by means of tableaux on one side of the stage, which only certain characters see. The scene is the house in Altona, a Hamburg suburb, of the von Gerlachs, Protestant industrial magnates.[26] Like the father (nicknamed by his children "Old Hindenburg"), it represents power. But old von Gerlach, who typifies the domineering authoritarianism Sartre associates with paternity, is dying of throat cancer. The disease is symbolic; the reference to the throat points to the importance of voices and speech, in this play and others. Moreover, his industrial empire has changed; owner-ship and management are becoming separate, and he no longer leads. This is one aspect of Sartre's dialectical understanding of capitalism, according to which it devours human freedom, as men's acts escape from them and become oppressive institutions. Before dying the father wishes to see his recluse elder son, Frantz,[27] closeted and tended only by his sister Léni, with whom he has an incestuous relationship. Direct requests are useless; Léni will not transmit them. The father appeals to Johanna, the beautiful wife of his second son, Werner, to act as his intermediary. The dynamics among these five characters, recalling the ceaseless conflicts in *Huis-clos,* are too complex for summary; at times one has the impression that the author is interested in perverted human relationships for themselves, beyond their function of representing contemporary civilization. Johanna, who wants to leave permanently, consents to see Frantz in the hope that von Gerlach, satisfied, will then release Werner from his oath to remain in the house forever. She is the least sequestered of all, the most fearful of being a prisoner; she alone sees through sham, including her own former artificial identity as a movie star. Werner, a fine physical specimen but weak in character, seems interested chiefly in trying to win from his father, tardily, the recognition he never received, as a younger son.

Living in the past, Frantz believes that Germany is still in ruins, after the defeat, and broods over the destruction caused by the war. He spends his time making tape-recorded speeches to plead the case of the twentieth century before the thirtieth, where the imaginary listeners are not human beings but crabs (men having destroyed themselves), who represent the judgment of the future on our century.[28] Léni helps him preserve the illusion of Germany's ruin, ostensibly to protect him, in truth because their love requires this illusion. His inability to adjust to postwar life reflects several sources of guilt. One is his father's responsibility for another's death. The old man had knowingly sold land for a concentration camp, and had been at least half responsible for turning over to the S.S. an escaped rabbi, whom Frantz had unsuccessfully hidden. Frantz himself feels guilty about this episode, for as the S.S. beat the rabbi to death under his eyes he felt a surge of complicity with them. (Sartre suggests that his humanitarianism was abstract and idealistic—a reaction due to Lutheran influence—and that actual violence and hatred are always below the surface of bourgeois kindness.[29]) Frantz also feels guilt for having consented to torture peasant partisans on the Russian front. It is easy to see why in his eyes Germany must remain in ruins; its new prosperity (one aspect of "loser wins") would make defeat seem desirable and remove all justification for his compromises. While feeling guilt, however, and obviously seeking to expiate his crimes, Frantz also finds responsibility outside himself, in what he calls history. This is not just a scapegoat; nor is it fatalism, in the ordinary sense, when he says, "When our fathers got our mothers pregnant, they made soldiers" (142). Rather, it is the Marxist-based view that the political and economic circumstances in Europe were certain to produce violence and thus took away freedom.

As in "La Chambre," when Johanna visits Frantz repeatedly she begins to take on his madness, sharing his hallucinations and nearly consenting to sequester herself with him. This almost reverses the roles: coming to realize that she is destroying him by tearing down the refuge of his insanity, he recognizes his own aberrations. He eats his war medals, actually made of chocolate, thus acknowledging their fakery and German prosperity. As he and Johanna approach a mutual recognition which, in less perverted circumstances, would be love, he draws away from Léni. Yet he sees that they are instruments of torture to each other and that there is no way out from this moral imprisonment. Léni, not to be ignored, destroys their precarious understanding by revealing to Johanna that Frantz had condoned torture. He thus loses both his lunacy and his one mediation with reality. At the conclusion of the fourth act, he agrees to meet with his father.[30]

The fifth act is the confrontation of two generations with each other and truth. Here as elsewhere, the play smacks of the bourgeois drama that Sartre wished to deny. But what is at stake is not just family conflict, but the moving forces of history itself. To their recognition of mutual guilt, father and son can find one answer only, suicide. They drive Léni's car at a dangerous speed around the river bends. When the others realize the inevitable outcome of this, Léni announces she will go cloister herself, replacing Frantz. Johanna and Werner are left to a future which can be considered open. The play is somewhat circular, like *Huis-clos* and *Nekrassov*, yet there has been change, including a suggestion that Johanna, more in need of authenticity than the others, might force Werner to leave the family business, thus breaking their tie to destructive capitalism. At the conclusion, Frantz's taped voice reads his indictment of the century and of the cruel, flesh-eating beast that is man.

It is probably appropriate to see World War II atrocities as standing for French brutality in Algeria. Yet the references to Germany are apposite in themselves. The nation capable of the worst excesses is also the most prosperous in postwar Europe. Old von Gerlach explains that he had cooperated with the Nazi government because it was obtaining new markets for German industrial production, necessary for a rebuilt nation, after its crushing in the earlier war—itself the product of what Sartre considered a bankrupt colonialist capitalism. The connections among modern history, capitalism, and violence thus underlie the entire play (*TS*, 333–34). Indeed, if there is any answer to the question of why such evils exist, it is that capitalist expansionism will necessarily breed violence, which turns back upon its perpetrators like a monstrous creation, an "infernal machine" (107). This view, expressed at length in the elaborate dialectical arguments of the *Critique*, is also the key to the play.

Les Séquestrés d'Altona is considered by many critics as one of three major Sartrean dramas, along with *Huis-clos* and *Le Diable et le Bon Dieu*.[31] Each is connected to a major development in Sartre's thought. The third is the only literary expression of his major ideological effort to join Marxism with existentialism. It is also a reminder of many of his concerns. The incest motif, visible also in *Les Mots*, refers perhaps to his childhood.[32] Germany is a frequent reference point elsewhere in his thought, and the allusions to Luther recall his Protestant origins. Even the crabs, reminders of his own hallucinations, appear frequently elsewhere. Family skeletons and shameful personal secrets are a common motivation in his work, starting with *Les Mouches,* as are hostility to the father and the conflict between consciousnesses.

It is instructive to compare the play with *La Chute (The Fall)* by Camus, published in 1956. With the Algerian conflict in the background, though unmentioned, Camus by skillful argumentation draws his hero Clamence and the reader into a recognition of everyone's guilt and what he calls "sweet dreams of oppression."[33] He ends by showing the culpability of the whole century, and the impossibility of escaping responsibility even by self-judgment. It can be argued that his novel is more successful than Sartre's play. Whereas identification with Clamence is almost inevitable, and thus the *feeling* of guilt is shared, it is difficult to be touched by Sartre's characters. Identification was not, of course, what he wanted, but rather that Brechtian distance which nevertheless allows for recognition, as one would suddenly "recognize" in the savage mores of a primitive tribe one's own self (*WS,* 359). But the demands of this theatrical aesthetic may well prove too great, at least in the case of *Les Séquestrés.*

Les Troyennes

Sartre's last drama is an adaptation of Euripides' *Trojan Women,* performed in 1965. He had been impressed with the connection between an earlier translation of the work and the Algerian conflict.[34] Although peace had been achieved in 1962, the Indochinese War, of which he was an adamant opponent, was still in progress. He was also attracted to Euripides as the dramatist of the decline of Greek myth, when belief in the gods was waning, as the sense of human responsibility grew. Wishing to modernize the play sufficiently to make it palatable and meaningful to contemporary audiences and yet keep it properly formal and in perspective, he used free verse and a language that is fairly familiar, yet rarely vulgar, stylized enough to recall the nobility of Greek tragedy.

The Trojan War and its aftermath are the occasion for a general condemnation of war, as a human creation. As in Euripides, there is special indictment of colonial and imperialist domination. The chorus anachronistically mentions Europe and its colonial expansion and warfare in the name of civilization. "They told us then that they were bringing / Greek culture and European enlightenment / to the backward people of Asia" (49). A Greek emissary, announcing to Hecuba that Hector's shield will remain in Troy, to be used as a coffin for the child Astyanax, whom he has just had brutally slaughtered, observes, "We Europeans are both civilized /

and sensitive" (71). Like those in Montaigne's essay on cannibals and Mérimée's "Tamango," these brief comments have the effect of putting Occidental humanism into immediate perspective. But the most damning statement is Poseidon's final address to the "stupid, bestial mortals": "Can't you see / War / Will kill you: / All of you?" (80). To accuse the gods was the traditional position; as Sartre points out, Euripides lets his characters do so, but then shows that this is an evasion of what is really human responsibility. Hecuba's passionate accusations of divine wickedness, which ring with a modern note, have to be seen in light of Poseidon's statement. To Sartre there is no resolution within the play of this mutual accusation, and that is why it is tragic (see xv). But, beyond the play, man's total abandon or *délaissement* is not tragic but rather, as he has repeatedly said, simply the condition of his freedom.[35]

Sartre's final two dramatic works are just as pessimistic, in their way, as *Huis-clos* and other earlier plays. This should not be surprising, since, as the next chapter indicates, his philosophy, grounded increasingly in dialectical materialism, came to emphasize less man's entire (if unused) freedom and more his entrapment in a world where acts turn back on their agents and capture them in a network of magnified forces, beyond their control. He agreed that *Les Séquestrés* was his most somber drama. The stage does not allow for the argumentation needed to correct this pessimism by showing how history has other possibilities; in the *Critique,* he wrote no fewer than 750 pages on the topic. Sartre's theater, then, strikes one as generally negative, although *Les Mains sales* and *Le Diable et le Bon Dieu* point to some practical lines of action in a very imperfect world.

Chapter Seven
Criticism, Biographies, and Late Philosophy

Introduction

The critic dealing with Sartre primarily as an imaginative writer faces a dilemma when treating his later decades. On the one hand, his career as a novelist and dramatist was nearly complete by 1960,[1] and in *Les Mots* he denounced literature as an idol; his major existentialist works, to which his fiction and theater are closely related, had been written. On the other hand, under the impetus of the most crucial change of his life—his adoption of Marxism as the only valid modern philosophy—he produced major critical and political works. As he increasingly lent his prestige to radical causes both in France and elsewhere, his fame grew, and to some readers and in some perspectives his later works appear more important than his earlier ones. This may be true especially at the present time, since political conditions continue to resemble those he discussed. Consequently, whether or not the critic gives close attention to Sartre's last decades, the study is certain to seem unbalanced to those who would prefer a different emphasis. It is a problem which would not arise with a less complex and fertile figure. The solution adopted in the present case is to survey the production of his last period, without attempting to provide a lengthy assessment of every text, and without a close examination of his politics, impossible in a work of this scope. Before this survey is done, it is necessary to examine his earlier literary criticism, not previously considered.

Early Criticism

The canon of Sartre's criticism embraces art, literary, and biographic essays dating from the 1930s through the early 1970s.[2] Ironically, after Roquentin had condemned biography in *La Nausée,* Sartre devoted a number of years to it. The earliest examples of criticism are articles published mostly in the *Nouvelle Revue Française* and elsewhere, then collected in *Situations,* the first of a ten-volume series (1947–1976). Some of his most famous critical positions are set forth in these essays, the title of which is to be taken in its philosophic sense. For instance, his essay helped to establish Faulkner's position in France as an important innovator in technique and style, whose handling of fiction was appropriate to a modern conception of time. In Dos Passos he saw an equally radical innovator; the technique of such novels as *1919* made him hail the American as the greatest novelist of his time—a judgment he did not maintain in later years (*WS,* 60). In French fiction, he turned his attention to Mauriac, Giraudoux, and Camus. Summed up in his famous conclusion, "God is not an artist. Neither is M. Mauriac," his judgments on the first, whom he criticized for authorial manipulation, omniscience, and quasi-divine interventions, indicate his own aim of staying out of his novels and creating a sense of the characters' freedom.[3] Every student of Giraudoux is familiar with Sartre's interpretation of his fiction as presenting an Aristotelian view of the world, divided into neat categories and essences. Giraudoux is an essentialist, an anachronism in the modern world of becoming. On *L'Etranger (The Stranger)* of Camus, Sartre published a most sympathetic study of the style and characterization, which led him to see Meursault as a stranger to the world (like all human beings) as well as to society. Among other French writers treated are Paul Nizan, Denis de Rougemont, Maurice Blanchot, Francis Ponge, and Jules Renard. Among philosophers, he treats Descartes and Husserl.[4]

Sartre approaches the author through the text, not vice versa; historical and biographical considerations have little place. His criticism is generally directed toward what is essential in the writer's style, as it reveals his situation (see *C,* 268–71). A single novel, indeed one sentence in some cases, suffices to reveal to his phenomenologically oriented appreciation a writer's particular perspective, his understanding of space and time, his attitude toward his characters or his topic, his understanding of subjectivity and objectivity. Assuming, with Proust, that style is a question not of technique but of vision, or a conception of the world (*CRD,* 90), Sartre does not stop with noting a writer's peculiarities, but goes on to ask what these mean, and to show that they reveal a point of view, since man is the means by which reality is manifested. It is the same approach, magnified and enriched, which later produces his massive study of Flaubert.

"Qu'est-ce que la littérature?" (1947) in *Situations* II includes his most famous statements on committed literature, rooted in the politics of the time. Some of the views now seem dated, especially the assumptions that no political accommodation could be made between the United States and the Soviet Union and that Europe would soon be the battleground for an East-West war. But Sartre's understanding of literature as set forth here has permanent interest, and the text sheds considerable light on his own fiction of the late 1940s. He first distinguishes among the other fine arts, poetry, and prose. The former do not deal with significations; poetry does deal with them, but not with signs (for the poet, words are *things*); prose, dealing with signs, is by its nature utilitarian and engaged: to speak is to act. It is grounded in the writer's freedom and appeals by its essence to the freedom of its readers (since one cannot constrain a reader). This does not mean that its audience must be politically and economically free—quite the contrary—but that it is directed toward basic ontological freedom and must therefore, under penalty of denying its premises, take as its value and aim the realizing of this ontological freedom in practical terms; that is, the overcoming of alienation by means of socialist revolution. The art of prose is thus "liberal" and necessarily bound up with democracy. Just as, for Camus, art is always concerned with inner freedom and emancipation, Sartre contends that there can be no good literature of oppression, such as an anti-Semitic novel.[5] Moreover—and this view has important aesthetic implications—literature as freedom implies also the participation of the reader, who freely re-creates with the writer.

Sartre does not propose that literature be didactic; a thesis play, which presents a problem *and* a solution, is not what he urges, nor an aestheticism whereby the work itself *is* the solution, but instead an exploration of situations, with an appeal to reader and spectator as free to act for a solution. He is fully aware that this has not always been the relationship between writer and audience, and that literature has often been alienated. Indeed, his very interesting survey of the writer's position in France from the Middle Ages through the present shows that it has varied from subservience to Church, state, or an elite, as in the Middle Ages and seventeenth century, through revolutionary commitment on behalf of the rising bourgeoisie (during the Enlightenment, the period he prefers), to extreme antibourgeoisism and separation between the author and his public, to a contesting of literature itself in the twentieth century and a call for total destruction (surrealism), with simultaneously a reconciliation between the bourgeoisie and certain writers. He appeals for a new relationship, with new readers, neither the oppressive propertied classes, nor the proletariat (with whom no group of French writers has yet formed a relationship of any consequence), but intellectuals, professors, petty bourgeois, and others at the periphery. He looks ultimately for a classless literature, which will be totally freed, "the subjectivity of a society in permanent revolution" (159). In the meanwhile, he points out that the artist's utilization of contemporary media such as radio, cinema, and popular journalism is justified, and should be exploited to the point where public bad taste is reformed and the necessity of ending tyranny is compellingly visible. He stresses the need for a literature of praxis, "action in history and on history . . . a synthesis of historical relativity and moral and metaphysical absolute" appropriate to a socialist collectivity, the only place where literature can truly fulfill its function (239). However, he does not propose that the writer offer his services to the Communist party, which he condemns for being conservative in its means, though progressive in its ends, and which is incompatible with the honest exercise of literature. Sartre himself may have found this utopian program impractical: he later stated that he no longer believed in literature and its capacity to change men.[6] The basic view of literature as an appeal to freedom did not change, however, and the notion of praxis, writing as action in or on history, is consistent with his very historically oriented philosophy and criticism throughout the remainder of his career.

In the following eight volumes of *Situations,* which concern many other topics, mention should be made of essays on Nathalie Sarraute, Gide, Giacometti, Tintoretto (a favorite artist of Sartre's), Camus (including their last exchanges), Merleau-Ponty, and Kierkegaard, and comments on the New Novel, language, and prose versus poetry. The long essay on Nizan (*S* IV, 130–88) is especially interesting for its autobiographic material. There are also lengthy interviews and articles on colonialism and Algeria, including Sartre's preface to Frantz Fanon's *Les Damnés de la terre* (*The Wretched of the Earth*), the 1968 crisis in France, the American war in Vietnam, and Marxism. Especially noteworthy is the 1953 essay on Mallarmé, whom Sartre considered the greatest French poet (*S* IX, 14). He had long been interested in the author of *Igitur* and had composed on him a study of 500 pages, later lost (*WS,* 281); he returned to the topic frequently. His view of Mallarmé is highly unusual. He sees him as a committed writer—not to a particular political cause, to be sure, but to a new, anonymous literature, creating communion among the people, a sort of Orphic tragedy. According to Sartre, he was deeply revolutionary, contesting not a particular social structure but the whole world, from which he separated himself poetically, by a rival creation or rather poetic destruction of the world. He struggled against the materialistic view of the universe, which he found true, by attempting to create a literary absolute, while knowing that chance or determinism ("le hasard") could not be abolished by an act ("un coup de dés"). Sartre finally sees Mallarmé as announcing the modern period, living the death of God better than Nietzsche and, like Camus, considering suicide the only genuine question (*S* IX, 14–15, 191–200). These comments are noteworthy for the light they shed on Sartre's ability to draw an author to himself, making of one of France's greatest esthetes a hero and prophet of modern praxis.

Sartre's first monograph on a single author is his 1947 study of Baudelaire. Later he judged it as inadequate, even very bad (*S* IX, 113). It has been criticized for neglecting the artistic achievement of the poet, even tarnishing his greatness, and contributing nothing to the understanding of his verse, as well as for distortions. But since it was originally composed as an introduction to selections from his diaries and letters, its concentration on the eccentricities, neuroses, and sufferings of the man rather than on his poetry is reasonable. Moreover, it does shed light on themes recurrent in both his verse and prose, such as his guilt, fixation on certain embodiments of the feminine principle, and attraction to abjection and evil.[7] What Sartre attempts is what he calls existential psychoanalysis (already discussed in *L'Etre et le néant*), that is, a close study of the subject's character and behavior in light of his free choice about how and what to be, given his situation (not unlike Sartre's own, in this case). The self, it will be recalled, is not a given but a creation; there is no transcendent ego. As a clear challenge to Freudianism, the undertaking is a bold one.[8] The problem is to show, without recourse to determinism, how a person made determining decisions. The solution is the concept of original choice, made freely in childhood, which is at the origin of subsequent behavior; the latter is not *caused* by it unconsciously but rather freely adopted to be in conformity with it. The original choice is the subject's project, his resolution of his situation. In Baudelaire's case, it was the impossible project to *be* absolutely (as in-itself) while still existing (as for-itself) and remaining conscious of that being; that is, for his self to possess itself. He wanted to be a "freedom-thing." This need to be as if by divine right sprang from his early relationship with his mother; he sought to prolong his childhood, to deny the awful discovery (with his mother's remarriage) that his life was unjustified. It was thus a particular form of narcissism, in which he chose to live as another person, and whose modalities included solitude, originality, self-deprecation, filial dependence, need for authority, cult of the past, self-imposed suffering, metaphysical *ennui,* sexual reserve, dandyism, parasitism, cultivation of evil, and conservatism. The poet, a consummate actor, was permanently in bad faith (which does not exclude his lucidity); it was his way of concealing his freedom from himself and pretending to that inert being which he knew was impossible. Sartre's conclusion is that Baudelaire—like all men—had the life he deserved, since it was he who chose to live as he did in his situation.

The massive study of Jean Genet, *Saint Genet, comédien et martyr* (*Saint Genet, Actor and Martyr*), appeared in 1952. The title was borrowed from the Baroque dramatist Jean de Rotrou. Sartre originally projected his study as a preface; it became the 573-page introduction to Genet's works. Critics have noted how the fundamental dualism of good and evil on which it is based (already visible in *Baudelaire*) also furnishes the foundation for *Le Diable et le Bon Dieu,* presented the previous year. Genet and Goetz are both bastards, they look for absolutes, they play at "loser wins" (a motif in several other works also) and are fascinated by treason. Unlike the Baudelaire study, Sartre here conceives the man and the work as a totality, a dynamic synthesis. He wants to "show the limitations of psychoanalytic and Marxist explanations and [show] that only freedom can explain a person in his totality."[9] Again, the writer's behavior and work are seen as the function of an original choice he made in order to go beyond his situation. "The important thing is not what people make of us but what we make ourselves of what people make of us" (55). This is not intended as reductionist; rather, the autoanalysis the writer practiced was highly inventive and original as well as deliberately provocative; it was genius invented, and Genet is a modern hero.

Genet's original choice was made as a boy when he was caught stealing and called a thief. As a bastard and welfare child, he had no social status, no being granted him, unlike children of stable families, whether bourgeois or peasant, who have a sense of being right and justified. Lacking this, he was highly vulnerable to the judgment of others: judged as a thief, he felt himself to be one, and chose to assume this being in order to be his own cause. That is, he chose to make his new objectivity into a subjectivity, to interiorize it. His existence thus depended on the for-others. Henceforth his behavior was governed by this free assumption of his essence. It supposed a scale of values contrary to that of proper people but dependent upon it. Sartre analyzes elaborately and brilliantly, if too lengthily, the dialectics (that is, simultaneous affirmation and negation) of good and evil in Genet, their reflexivity, the relationship of doing to being, and how evil became his good and was interiorized, while yet remaining evil.[10] Arguing that Genet carried out his cult of evil more successfully than Baudelaire, he studies Genet's dimension of the sacred and has recourse to myth as both illustration and product of Genet's metamorphosis into a thief. He then analyzes Genet's role-playing, shows the connection between theft and homosexuality, studies the role of language, and shows the relationship of evil to literary creation, exploring the theme of art as Satanic which is visible in French literature from the Middle Ages through Baudelaire, Gide, and Mauriac. He demonstrates how the whole of Genet, from his sexual peculiarities to his choice of literary forms, images, and style, is a function of his choice, a self-creation by which he recuperated his alienated self. Again, it could be argued that this analysis contributes little to the understanding of Genet's work because it is too exclusively focused on the man, especially his sordid side. But the thematic structure of his works, the characters' relationships, their concern with appearances, and their ontological and psychological assumptions are ultimately illuminated by this analysis, which again rejects Freudian labels and concepts. One should note in passing the analysis of several poems of Genet—a rare example of Sartre as a poetry critic.

Saint Genet is more than an existentialist psychobiography, for unlike *Baudelaire* and the analyses in *L'Etre et le néant,* it examines the subject's freedom in relationship to the objective situation, as it is conditioned by it. Without completely abandoning his position on freedom, Sartre qualifies it by seeing it as alienated, by oneself or society, especially through economic and hierarchical structures. Although this perspective is Marxist, he does not accept Marxist determinism but rather argues that free choice within a situation is the only satisfactory explanation for the creation of a certain man and work. Thus he attempts the synthesis of existentialist and Marxist positions which later forms the basis for major writings. *Saint Genet* is thus a pivotal work previewing later criticism, as well as a brilliant analysis.[11]

Autobiography

Sartre's next subject is himself, in *Les Mots,* composed mostly from 1954 on, then revised and published in 1963 (magazine form) and 1964 (see *C,* 274–76). His self-portrait was an outgrowth of his crisis of the 1950s, which led to his self-questioning and his reevaluation of literature as a way of life, a project or effort to be. By 1954, he almost regretted having chosen literature (*WS,* 430). He said in 1955 that the work would "define myself in relationship to the historical situation, utilizing as a system of investigation a certain psychoanalysis as well as the Marxist method."[12] Critics have noted that the *Critique de la raison dialectique* provides the theoretical framework for situating this work.[13] Like several other famous autobiographies, it is autoanalysis, a study in the solutions he found to the problems of his childhood situation. However, it is not an apology but an accusation—a poignant and at times indulgent one, to be sure,[14] but an indictment nonetheless—of his childish and mature idolatry of words (following Charles Schweitzer's example), which are substitutes for reality, the stuff of roles, to which he clutched as a justification for his life, which otherwise seemed to him, as Roquentin said, given for nothing. Yet he treats himself as a child with humor, thereby expressing the distance between that child and himself now.[15] In its rhetorical nature and its attempt to draw a lesson, albeit a negative one, from his life, the work resembles those autobiographies which William L. Howarth has called "oratorical," while sharing also "poetic" features because of the casting of the characters in varied, and perhaps highly stylized, roles.[16] The book is also one of the many Sartrean attacks on the bourgeoisie, whose early and awful influence alienated him and distorted his outlook, he thought, for decades. Alive with superb characterizations of his family and others—although he said he wanted to avoid the anecdotic and novelistic, and instead define his relationship to the historical situation (*WS,* 429)—it is an outstanding, if acerbic, portrait of the French and Alsatian bourgeoisie in the early years of the century, whose idealism, Sartre suggested, spoiled a whole generation of men like himself (*WS,* 428). It is the "myth of a Messiah-writer of a dechristianized bourgeoisie which Sartre demolishes in *Les Mots.*"[17]

Sartre's thesis, already illustrated in *Saint Genet,* is that one is not born with genius—at most, with capacities. Rather, one makes himself into a genius in the course of seeking, and creating, solutions to certain problems. Thus he stresses both conditioning and freedom within conditioning. He emphasizes the milieu, however, much more than in *Baudelaire.* That his childhood, while seemingly happy and certainly protected, posed problems to the developing boy, no one will question; that the child had to adapt in some way, whether destructively or constructively, seems equally obvious. What *Les Mots* leaves unexplained is why Sartre's original choice to live for and by words should lead not just to his neurosis, which he acknowledges, but to the brilliance, originality, and perceptiveness which make of him a major philosophic and creative writer. He has said that intelligence is always the product of a situation (*S* IX, 80), but why some react more intelligently than others to their alienation is not clear.[18]

Sartre concludes in a disabused tone that he has never escaped from his original choice, made in response to his situation; that he still likes heights, still lives his neurosis or, rather, his chosen self, and, without believing in literature as an absolute, still writes pages and pages—supreme irony—as if to please his long-dead grandfather, who could not have approved of his vocation, still less of his political opinions (*W*, 101). One does not escape from oneself, he concludes; only the belief underlying these habits is gone. It sounds like the fatigue and disappointment of an aging, blasé man, and critics have taken the book to be his final word, the expression of a failure.[19] But this is not the case since, during the same years it was composed, he poured an astounding energy into the *Critique de la raison dialectique,* an effort to furnish a new departure for dialectical thinking, and so contribute to a new society. His self-criticism, then, was not a conclusion but a beginning.

Les Mots is a splendid, if tendentious, piece of autobiographical writing, full of insights and a sense of what a self is in existentialist terms. One can reasonably ask, as Francis Jeanson does, what portion of it is true, that is, a childhood really lived, and what part a reconstruction dictated by later perspectives (*SV*, 31–32). There is some of both, surely, in a somewhat dialectical relationship. It is also a work of art that denounces the work of art. It may be asked why he wrote so well a text destined to deflate literature. He explained that as a farewell to literature it is "an object which contests itself [and] should be written as well as possible" (*S* X, 94; *SH*, 89). It is complemented by other autobiographic material, chiefly interviews, including a long one published in *Situations* X, detailed conversations with Beauvoir (*C*, 165–559), and the text of a film, "Sartre par lui-même," published as *Sartre* (*Sartre by Himself*). These are not a continuation of his formal memoirs, which stop in mid-childhood, but rather spontaneous reminiscences and judgments. He also wanted to add to his memoirs a sort of "political testament" (*WS*, 430; *S* IX, 134); his interviews come closest to this. In the next years there will probably be much personal material among the unpublished texts coming to light, such as the "Journal de Mathieu" in *Les Temps Modernes* (September 1982) and his *Carnets* (1983). (Another text which would be welcome to critics is his long unpublished study on Nietzsche [C, 234]). While he denied having a literary correspondence of consequence (*S* X, 209), Beauvoir describes his letters as lively, immediate, and worth publishing (*C*, 228–29).

L'Idiot de la famille

Sartre's study of Flaubert is his last effort at existential psychoanalysis, combined with the Marxist viewpoints and dialectical methods which are also basic to the *Critique de la raison dialectique.* Although the latter antedates the Flaubert study by eleven years, it will be examined out of chronological sequence so that all the critical biographies can be considered together. This does not distort the study of *L'Idiot,* since both it and the *Critique* follow the same methodology and are based on the same assumptions; in fact, Sartre said he wrote the *Critique* in order to prepare for studying Flaubert (*S* IX, 11). Moreover, as Robert Champigny has observed, the Flaubert study, which Sartre called a "true novel" (*S* X, 94)—that is, drawing on the imagination as well as biographical information—is related not only to earlier critical works but also to the early philosophy, acquaintance with which is necessary to comprehend it.[20] It consists of three large volumes; the fourth, which was to be a study of the style in *Madame Bovary,* was never written.

Sartre's choice to devote the last years of his productive life, particularly of his failing eyesight, to this massive critical biography of a neurotic, antibourgeois writer who was still very bourgeois may be explained in part by the resemblances between them. He may also have remained fascinated by the ogre of the bourgeoisie and wished to chastise it again. He admits not liking Flaubert and venting some of his dislike on the family, but denies any personal grievance, since his own childhood was happy and his mother very affectionate (*S* X, 96–97). He had been interested in the nineteenth-century writer even as a child and especially after reading his correspondence during World War II; several previous works use him as an example. The biography was the result of a sort of competition between him and the Communist critic Roger Garaudy: around 1955 they agreed that each would write on a famous figure, the one according to existentialist methods, the other by Marxist methods; the results would then be compared (*S* X, 91–92). He labored on the study in 1955 and then between 1968 and 1970; it was published in 1971 and 1972. Unlike other works whose promised sequels had never appeared, he was determined to conclude it; only poor sight prevented its completion.

Illustrating his Marxist-existentialist approach to a concrete problem via dialectical reason,[21] the study proposes to interpret known facts and, extrapolating from these, to create imaginatively the areas of Flaubert's biography, such as his infancy, which have not been recorded. Focusing on what he calls the *vécu* or lived (a term which partially replaces *consciousness*) (*S* X, 95), he attempts to explain how and why the second son of Dr. Achille Flaubert became a passive, neurotic partisan of art for art's sake and great novelist. His aim is, however, less to inform the reader about Flaubert than to illustrate what can be known of a man in a certain context (assuming basic factual information is available) by his method, which challenges the traditional understanding of character in French literature and psychology, derived from seventeenth-century understanding of human nature and motivation. He especially wishes to demonstrate that knowing a man implies a dialectical understanding of his milieu—not an analytical or causal understanding, as in the nineteenth-century view that the milieu produces the man, but rather the supposition that the one reflects the other, each acting and reacting on the other in a relationship that is both positive and negative. He also relies heavily on psychoanalysis, but attempts to avoid the mechanistic aspect of Freudian interpretations, and contends that *le vécu* is "life in understanding with itself, without knowledge or thetic consciousness being indicated" (*C,* 19). He calls his method, visible already in *Les Mots,* progressive-regressive; he looks backward, as does the psychoanalyst, but uses the results of this investigation to look forward to the progression of Flaubert's development, toward a synthetic act which is always explained in terms of its end (see *CRD,* 91, 96). The approach is thus teleological, assuming a necessary relationship between Flaubert's behavior and an end, dimly seen and yet necessary.

The biography begins with a methodological statement and a study of Flaubert's family and early childhood: the domineering, successful, positivistic father, the favored elder brother, the unaffectionate mother, and uncomfortable little Gustave, who did not learn to read (thus an "idiot") until at age seven his father forced him to become literate. This situation is the source of Flaubert's original choice, not that to become a writer, which comes much later, but to define himself as secondary to his father and brother, valuing only what they did not value, and to remain passive and oppressed—to live in unhappiness and, like the whole bourgeoisie, which he incarnated in spite of himself, to alienate his freedom. The portrait of his adolescence is followed by close examination of his famous attack at Pont-l'Evêque, which "proved" to his family that he could not live in the utilitarian world, and thus constituted a victory over his father without his ever having overtly challenged paternal authority. This confirmed his existence as an artist, in the nonutilitarian world of the imaginary. In the third volume, Sartre treats Flaubert's neurosis as a function of his time, moving from the subjective realm to the objective one and studying the whole period, in an attempt "to explain how the contradictions of this world in Marxist terms are internalized in an individual," that is, how Flaubert's neurosis reflects that of the entire period.[22]

It will take years for critics to digest the richness of this study, which Serge Doubrovsky has called an "anthropological saga," and to assess its contribution to Flaubert studies and Marxist-existentialist psychoanalysis

(*WS,* 570). A sample of critical reaction today would reveal on the one hand enthusiasm, on the other annoyance with Sartre's "Germanic" style and criticism of his lack of originality.[23] What is most important to keep in mind, perhaps, is the dual stress in *L'Idiot* on freedom and conditioning. As Sartre came increasingly to see that theoretical freedom was alienated more often than not, he grew correspondingly interested in the process of alienation (whether by economics, class, or family) and the attempts of consciousness to deal with this alienation, whence the great role played by the environment and reigning ideology in all his studies of writers. In Flaubert's case, he wished to show that the boy's options were conditioned by his special family situation and the objective situation of the bourgeoisie and its ideology in France in the early nineteenth century; how Gustave interiorized these and then went beyond them by means of creation in the imaginary is the story of how Flaubert became an artist.

Critique de la raison dialectique

The second of Sartre's major philosophic works was begun in 1957 and published in 1960. It reflects his crucial and profound encounter with Marxism, which he considered the only valid philosophy and method for this century, not to be surpassed as long as the circumstances that gave rise to it, principally scarcity, dominate human relations (*CRD,* 30–32). Its assumptions and analyses shed considerable light on such works as *Saint Genet, Les Mots,* and *Les Séquestrés d'Altona.* Its connection to *L'Idiot de la famille* is organic, entire sections having been transferred from one study to the other; and the whole of Sartre's later career is illuminated by its 755 dense pages. Although the promised second volume was never completed and published, the work is considered by many a major twentieth-century text.[24]

The study, which can be broadly described as a Marxist-existentialist study of history and society, originated in 1957 when a Polish journal requested Sartre to do an article on existentialism. After writing it, he realized its inadequacy; he recognized that he needed to establish a methodological base and describe the scope and validity of dialectics (*S* IX, 11). The book's title states clearly his aim: perform for dialectical reasoning, in an existentialist framework, what Kant did for analytical reason, showing its scope and capabilities and in particular proving to current Marxists that their use of the dialectical method was static, their position too monistic. Sartre draws on other disciplines to complete and support his

study, especially history, Freudian psychology, which the Marxists ne-
glect, and anthropology. In fact he conceives of his work as an anthropology, though he rejects the theses of what has become structuralist anthropology.[25] The use of psychoanalysis (without the terminology and
rigidity of much Freudianism) is partly a compensation for having ne-
glected, in his early philosophy, the valuable contributions of that discipline, partly an effort to make modern Communists see it as valuable
rather than as another expression of bourgeois decadence. Similarly, he
tries to show that the existentialist perspective is useful to Marxism, rather
than a contradiction of it. His intention is, in short, synthetic, as is his
progressive-regressive or analyticosynthetic method, which consists of
analysis of the historical singularity of the object, then a synthesis which
replaces the object in the whole historical or biographical process, via
"reciprocal enveloping" (CRD, 87, 93–94).[26]

Dialectics in the traditional sense, as used by Plato and Aristotle, refers
to logical reasoning, disputation, and argumentation, including the use of
analysis. Hegel gave the term its modern meaning by asserting that all
dialectic proceeds by a necessary development through thesis, antithesis,
and synthesis, toward an absolute. He then applied this pattern to the
development of history, thus raising to a level of universal idealism what
had begun as a logical method, a tool of the mind. Applying Hegel's
pattern to his understanding of historical change, in a materialist instead
of an idealist framework, Marx created dialectical materialism, a method
of historical analysis based on the theses that human beings, by their
economic needs, indirectly produce their form of life, that is, the mode of
production dominates all cultural and historical development, and that
this conditioning creates opposing forces in a dialectical movement—
negations and contradictions, resolutions, totalizations. Sartre accepted
these theses but accused contemporary Marxists of having misunderstood
or ossified them and of being blind to events.

Dialectics, Sartre asserts, is opposed to mere analytical reason, which is
reductive, causal, and thus linear—one thing leading to another and then
to a third in a simple, direct order. Indeed, it is so opposed that anyone
who limits himself to analysis cannot even understand dialectics, which he
defines as "the absolute intelligibility of an irreducible novelty *insofar as*
the latter is an irreducible novelty" (CRD, 147; Sartre's emphasis). He
puts on trial the French tradition of analytical reasoning for having limited
him and generations of French to a Cartesian view of the world, making it
impossible for him to understand Freud and Marx without a complete
reeducation; his own early work, he acknowledges, is marred by this flaw.

Nevertheless, dialectical reasoning *includes* analysis, and integrates it into a synthesis; it is "the control of analysis in the name of a totality" (*S* IX, 76).

Dialectics is thus the means of intelligibility of wholes—the total act and its "pluridimensional unity," the total man (as in *L'Idiot*), within the total group, within the total society (*CRD*, 74, 175). These are all defined in relation to each other within the totality of human history. Only by seeing collectivities or "ensembles" as totalities, Sartre asserts, can one understand a person, a system, or a structure. It is necessary to distinguish between totality and totalization (*CRD*, 138). Totality is latent or virtual; as early as *L'Etre et le néant* Sartre spoke of a "detotalized totality," which, in its widest sense, would be the world or the whole of phenomena: God's nonexistence means that there is no one outside the system to do the addition and create the totality. Even small totalities are normally detotalized. Totalization is the synthetic process, never complete, since reality is recurrent, by which a potential totality is realized, whether intellectually or practically, through a dynamic process of becoming. It is "the individual thinking and acting."[27] "With Hegel, Sartre holds that history and institutions show a dialectic development . . . a growth ('totalization') governed by the action and reaction of consciousness."[28] Truth itself is a "totalization which is ceaselessly totalized; particular facts mean nothing, are neither true nor false, as long as they have not been related, by the mediation of different partial totalities, to the totalization in process" (*CRD*, 30). In historical terms, totalization would be the classless society, no longer analytically divided, but a unity, in which the individual would no longer be separate. In rhetorical terms, it is the product of dialectical reasoning; dialectics is "the very movement of totalization, its intelligibility" (*CRD*, 139). One can suggest even a theological analogy, the *eschatos*, the end of historical time. Throughout the *Critique*, Sartre's aim is to lead the reader by one dialectical process after another to an understanding of totalities—especially historical collectivities—not so much in order to rewrite history as to illustrate the possibilities of dialectical reasoning, or "to establish the critical foundations of Marxist historical materialism by examining the *formal* conditions of possibility and intelligibility of the dialectic of History" (*WS*, 371; Sartre's emphasis).

History, then, is considered as a detotalized totality, "a totalization which temporalizes itself" (*CRD*, 144), which the philosopher attempts to understand. (Sartre distinguishes understanding from knowing: understanding is interior, a totalizing movement which gathers the subject and his environment into a synthetic unity [*CRD*, 97].) What causes history and how does it operate? The familiar Marxist answers are rigorously mechanistic and deterministic: economic and social processes take place in a dialectical development in a necessary fashion, from material causes alone, and which includes the struggle of opposing classes, the downfall of some and rise of others. Negative elements are embraced by positive, so that even resistance to history is instrumental in bringing it about. Man is thus a passive product. Rejecting this complete determinism, Sartre criticizes Marxism for labeling as chance all the concrete determinations of human life and retaining only the "abstract universal skeleton" of historical totalization (CRD, 58). He wants to allow for human consciousness and freedom, on which his earlier existentialism was based, and which he defines as "the irreducibility of the cultural order to the natural order" (CRD, 96). In particular, he wishes to discover, as in studying Flaubert, "the mediations which permit one to engender the singular concrete, life . . . the person from the *general* contradictions of productive forces and relationships of production" (CRD, 45; Sartre's emphasis). Refusing to reduce it to chance or reduce being to knowing, he insists upon the specificity of the event (CRD, 82, 122). He quotes Engels: "Men make their history themselves but in a given milieu which conditions them" (CRD, 60). Retaining something of the notion of intentionality, he stresses human action on, relationship to, and treatment of the material, not just the material itself. Man is still characterized, as in L'Etre et le néant, as a singular project, a going-beyond (CRD, 63).

There is, however, some change in the understanding of man, who, in the earlier philosophy, was autonomous, complete freedom from definition. Here, the individual, defined as "a practical organism living with a multiplicity of fellows in a field of scarcity" (CRD, 688), is seen as a socioeconomic product first, a consciousness second.[29] In this context, to be free means to pursue an action arising from need and going beyond material conditions in view of a precise objective (CRD, 441). This pursuit is carried out by means of the body, through praxis (a notion borrowed from Marx), which is in its original form work—"instrumentalization of material reality," or the dialectical negation of matter as it is reorganized in view of a future objective, to fulfill a need (CRD, 231, 370). Praxis is elsewhere defined as "an organizing project going beyond material conditions towards an end and inscribing itself through work in inorganic matter as an altering of the practical field and a reunification of means in view of attaining the end" (CRD, 687). Praxis is free action in and on the world; it is history. It can even be called man himself, "an organism which reproduces its life by reorganizing its environment" (*CRD*, 367), sometimes merely by its presence rather than by conscious activity. As Wilfrid Desan writes, "The concrete existent, which . . . was called freedom, project, and Being-for-itself, becomes in the semantics of the *Critique* praxis, or conscious activity of the individual."[30]

Need is the first totalizing relationship between man and the material complex around him. Scarcity of material to fill human needs is the most important determinant conditioning our relationship to the material, and explains fundamental human structures (techniques and institutions). It is the negative unity of human beings. It is a fact of humanity and not of nature. Because of scarcity, every human being is a threat to every other, since each can take what another needs; the risk of death is the original relationship of men through the mediation of matter (*CRD*, 689). Work, it has been seen, is the totalization of the environment (as a field of utensility) with a view toward fulfilling need. Unfortunately, it cannot always produce what is needed, for lack of materials, lack of tools, other incompatibility between means and ends, or additional reasons. This creates struggle, which Sartre no longer attributes to the desire of one consciousness for the death of the other, but the effort to remedy scarcity. If scarcity disappeared, basic human relations would change: man would no longer be man. Human reciprocity is modified in such a way that the other appears as an enemy, a fellow and yet radically different. With the advent of industrialization, the problem of scarcity has been exacerbated rather than solved; it appears less and less contingent and more generated by men themselves. No real progress is possible as long as scarcity continues to dominate praxis, as in the continued undernourishment of most of the world's population; as *Les Séquestrés d'Altona* suggests, warfare and other violence will remain characteristic as long as the economic system is one of exploitation. Men are not free under such a system. "Men are all slaves insofar as their vital experience unfolds in the field of the practico-inert and in the specific measure in which this field is originally conditioned by scarcity" (*CRD*, 369).

The practico-inert, a basic concept, is matter constituting itself as a negation of praxis, objectifying human agents and alienating freedom. It is the domain to which belong "social objects" such as collectivities; it also includes language, mass media, public opinion, currency, etc.[31] It implies the "coefficient of adversity" of matter, an aspect of the resistance of the environment (*BN*, 482). Moreover, history, beginning as free action, appears to contain a mechanical or antisocial element, escaping from and going beyond human freedom, producing what Sartre calls "counter-finalities." Why this is so is one of his greatest concerns. Dialectics reveals history turning back on those who initiate it, becoming an unrecognizable force, objectifying man, who was originally subject, and alienating his freedom. History thus has retroactive power and creates an "anti-humanity" or "anti-praxis" parallel to the "anti-physis" (a rearranged nature) created by man. "Inorganic materiality closes in on human multiplicity and transforms producers into its product" (*CRD*, 375). This creates historical necessity. For Sartre, alienation plays a role comparable to that Marx assigns it, but it is no longer just work which is alienated but the basic freedom which, *L'Etre et le néant* showed, is human reality. The example of Chinese peasants who deforested the land in order to plant it is apt: "The worker becomes his own material fatality; he produces the floods which ruin him" (*CRD*, 234). This is not because man does not make history, but because the *other* also makes it (*CRD*, 61). Additional illustrations are the introduction into France of British machines, and the "coal-iron complex" in England, where the development of new techniques, instead of allowing for general prosperity, turned into a negation of the greater number, in the form of expropriation and proletarization of the English peasantry. Another case, which Sartre affirms would be incomprehensible through analytic reason, is the flow of gold from the New World into sixteenth-century Spain, along with new techniques for mining and handling it. At first, these enriched the country, but the "behavior" of gold did not conform to the original aim of creating wealth: abundance turned into negativity, through rising prices, bankruptcy of merchants, increased impoverishment of the common people, and the drain of gold out of Spain.

Collectivities, to which Sartre accords lengthy attention, include series, in which the relationship between members is only formal and logical (e.g., people waiting for the bus, or all the drivers in Paris), fused groups, defined as "a synthetic relationship uniting men for an act and by an act" (*CRD*, 416), which are in opposition to, but can become, the third type, built on an oath or pledge, whose foundations, no matter what the form or circumstances, are terror and fraternity. The group is produced by "the project of tearing away from wrought matter its inhuman power of mediation among men to give it, within the community, to each and all and to constitute itself, as structured, as taking back in hand the materiality of the practical field (things and collectivities) by free *communized praxis*" (*CRD*, 638). It is not only an instrument but a mode of existence, as the free milieu of free human relations, producing, on the basis of the oath, man as a free individual; again, Sartre's italics indicate his stress on the relationship between institution and praxis, when he writes that the group is "the most effective *means* of governing surrounding materiality in the framework of scarcity and the *absolute end* as pure freedom freeing men from otherness" (*CRD,* 639). Sartre explains the overcoming of the alienation of seriality, which creates the fused group, and the subsequent process of turning a fused group into the pledged one, which is the ideal means of mass action, and may in some ways be compared to the general will of Rousseau. He then describes the *organization* of the group and considers such structures as classes and institutions, including the state and the concept of sovereignty. It is noteworthy that he criticizes bureaucratization (which arises when seriality threatens the group) in both capitalist societies and socialist ones, and in passing shows how the idea of the dictatorship of the proletariat is absurd (*CRD,* 630). The lengthy discussions, which occupy most of the middle and end of the *Critique,* of series, fused groups, organized and institutionalized groups, cannot be summarized here; their sociological value will not be completely assessed for a long time, although some have already questioned it, for instance, the noted anthropologist Claude Lévi-Strauss. Sartre's conclusions are that bourgeois intellectualism, which is class-based and yet has pretensions to universality (for instance, in its understanding of man), and which excludes the workers as subhuman, rests on analytical reason, and thus the rise of the proletariat must be based on dialectical reason and the creation of a new universal. Ultimately, praxis and dialectics are identical, and the class conflict is a conflict of rationalities. Dialectics is finally "a practical awareness of an oppressed class fighting against its oppressor"; it is the "objective spirit" of the working class, and by its nature antagonistic, as long as human relationships remain on a foundation of scarcity (*CRD,* 741–44).

By the time he composed the *Critique,* which Francis Jeanson calls the most profound modern study of the relationship to others as the fabric of history (*SV,* 135), and the Flaubert study, Sartre had obviously progressed very far from his idealistic phenomenological position, which stresses ontological freedom and the individual as for-itself, almost ignoring the social context, recognizing only the for-others. His adoption of Marxism marked a break with much of his own writing as well as his class. Fascinated with treason (like Genet and Goetz), he seems predisposed toward negation, perhaps especially against himself.[32] Although contradiction is an important step in dialectics and self-accusation is practiced by both Communists and Christians, to have come so far from his point of departure is noteworthy. Yet such themes as freedom, inauthenticity or alienation, generalization or totalization, the role of others, and time as a human creation remain as constants in his thought and provide continuity through three decades of philosophical writing.

Chapter Eight
Conclusion

Sartre believed that the twentieth century had a responsibility going beyond that of any previous epoch—the total responsibility to create man. Throughout history the human species has remained as Frantz described it in *Les Séquestrés d'Altona:* the hairless beast that kills its own kind, a "meat-eating, cruel, intelligent species" (*CRD,* 208). Humanism is a farce, and religious and ethical systems merely legitimize hierarchization and oppression; as he showed, for instance, in the *Critique,* the Church in the sixteenth century, by syphoning off value (in the form of gold), contributed to scarcity rather than relieving it. Faithful to the spirit of *L'Etre et le néant,* Sartre assumed that some freedom remains, even if it is conditioned and alienated by more refined systems of oppression than ever before; he also believed that recent historical developments have made it clear that this freedom must be exercised now, lest the final chance for humanity be missed. The responsibility is not just collective; it is individual. He insisted throughout his career that there is no innocent bystander: he who does not protest and attempt to stop injustice is just as responsible as the perpetrator. He judged his most important works— those which should be read *now*—to be political ones: *Situations, Saint Genet,* the *Critique,* and *Le Diable et le Bon Dieu,* although *La Nausée* was the most successful from a strictly literary point of view (*S* X, 155; *C,* 215). Since descriptions of man's increased technological capacities for self-destruction are commonplace, there is no need to evoke them in detail to make Sartre's position comprehensible. In any case, his emphasis is not on technology but on economic and political oppression, especially the domination of the third world by Western capitalism. This oppression is such that it has accomplished nearly total alienation of freedom, for both oppressors and oppressed alike. To combat it, the only arm is violence, the violence of the oppressors turned back upon them: nonviolence is foolish and ineffective, like Goetz's will to do nothing but good; besides, the violence of the proletariat is a counterviolence. After having so long been a subject, European man is becoming an object; he is being acted upon rather than acting, and this will replace the colonization of former decades.

Sartre's voice resembles that of the great Christian reformers, calling to repentance and evoking dreadful punishments for misdeeds, while assuming both the freedom of those addressed to change their nature and the ineluctable wrath of God, or, in his case, history. Octavio Paz has pointed out that, like Calvin and other reformers, his vision turns on the opposition between one's situation (predestination) and freedom.[1] It does not reveal, however, divine retribution but rather the imminent destruction through armed struggle of the hairless species and the opportunity perhaps lost for all time to create a race of men—what Sartre calls a unity of reciprocities—without any secrets, any distance between their interior and exterior, their subjectivity and objectivity, without ranks and hierarchies, struggle, rivalry, and fear—totally free in fact as well as potentiality, identical to themselves, and living in anarchy, or a society without powers (*S* X, 142–44, 156). This vision recalls the myth of the Golden Age, especially in the form Rousseau gives it, except that Sartre, unlike his predecessor, looks backward to no time in history or prehistory when man was fully himself; he assumes no human nature which has been corrupted. Rather, the new creation will be entirely future, and for it, in the most conscious century of all as well as the most methodically cruel, we are responsible: there is no mediator or heavenly age.

Sartre's eschatology is scarcely less visionary than that of St. John. True, he proposed immediate action and supported concrete stands on individual issues, but these cannot be considered as other than preliminary, and the creation of a new species seems, even in his writing, infinitely distant. He admits not being able to imagine what a new order would be like, suggesting only that it might involve exercise of authority by representatives of the proletariat (*SV*, 296). He bridges the gap between today's situation and the future by a kind of leap, not that of faith in man (since, true to Roquentin's spirit, he abhors man as he is), nor of idealism in the ordinary sense (his whole career was an effort to demolish it), but of visionary dialectics, since only it makes such a new creation even conceivable. Looking back—by what he would call the retrospective error if one analyzes it causally, or, as he would prefer, by dialectical understanding—one can see his whole career as the development of his rejection of God, his discovery of man's unjustified freedom and total responsibility, his encounter with alienation, and his application of these discoveries to contemporary history and society in a Marxist framework, by what Jeanson identifies as a constant moral concern and a developed, if subverted, sense of public service (*SV,* 263, 286). Like Rousseau, he is an incorrigible moralist; like Nietzsche, he is one of the great voices of atheism; with Hegel he shares a view of history as a synthetic process; like Marx, he sees it as a function of economics. He thus appears as an outstanding descendant and heir of some of the most prophetic and creative voices of the past two centuries. The twenty-first century will determine how great he appears in our own.

Notes and References

Chapter One

1. The biographical data in this chapter come from various sources, the most important of which (*SH, SV, W, WS,* and books by Beauvoir) are listed in the table of abbreviations and are indicated by parenthetical references. Unless specified otherwise, the principal dates and other facts are available in *WS,* 3–32 and passim (see its index) and in the excellent chronology which precedes Sartre's *Œuvres romanesques,* ed. Michel Contat and Michel Rybalka (Paris, 1981), pp. xxxvi–civ and will not be documented in the text. Since most of the Beauvoir volumes do not contain indexes—a major flaw—numerous page references are given to them to enable the reader to pursue his research. See *SV* for information on the marriage of Sartre's parents and *W* for other facts about his family.

2. For a psychoanalysis of Sartre's interpretation, see A. James Arnold and Jean-Pierre Piriou, *Genèse et critique d'une autobiographie: "Les Mots" de Jean-Paul Sartre,* Archives des Lettres Modernes, no. 144 (Paris: Minard, 1973), p. 29.

3. Philip Thody, *Sartre: A Biographical Introduction* (New York: Scribner's, 1971), pp. 15–16, 18.

4. *SH,* 11–12; *W,* 158; *C,* 367–69, 394–98, 409–11, 414–16; Jean-Paul Sartre, *Les Mots* (Paris: Gallimard, 1964), p. 85. A phrase in the original is mistranslated into English.

5. See Sartre's analysis of the situation in *SV,* 21, 269 ff., *SH,* 16, and *C,* 545 ff.

6. *SV,* 289–90. Thody thinks this is plausible (pp. 24–25).

7. Axel Madsen, *Hearts and Minds: The Common Journey of Simone de Beauvoir and Jean-Paul Sartre* (New York, 1977), p. 39; Arthur C. Danto, *Jean-Paul Sartre* (New York, 1975), p. 164; see also Sartre's preface to Paul Nizan's *Aden Arabie,* in *S* IV, 160–61, and *C,* 186, 373, 444.

8. This is comparable to Gide's conviction that his whole life was determined by the time he was in his twenties, indeed earlier. Sartre wrote an autobiographic sequel but did not publish it. See *SH,* 88; *S* IX, 133–34.

9. *SH,* 25; *C,* 205; *PL,* 44, which indicates that in 1929 a volume by Jean Wahl gave Sartre a few glimpses of Hegel. In *CRD,* 34, Sartre indicates that he read Husserl, Heidegger, and Jaspers for the first time in Berlin. On Marx, see *S* X, 191.

10. *SH,* 14, 17–19; *C,* 167, 247 ff. See also index to *MD.*

11. See *C,* 370–92, 399–401, for a long discussion of Sartre's relationships with women, and also *SH,* 23–24; *PL,* 65–66.

12. *SH,* 50; *C,* 222–23. See Marius Perrin, *Avec Sartre au stalag 12D* (Paris: Jean-Pierre Delarge, 1980), and Alfred R. Desautels, "The Sartre of Stalag 12D (1940–1941)," *French Review* 55, no. 2 (December 1981):201–6.

13. *S* X, 196; *C,* 341–45, 549; Germaine Brée, *Camus and Sartre* (New York: Dell, 1972).

14. Commenting on the position of a Marxist who is well-to-do, Beauvoir asserts there is no contradiction (*FC,* 652).

15. *FC,* 546. For comments on Sartre's attitude toward violence and justification of its use, see *S* V, 167–93, *CRD* passim, and Benny Lévy, "The Last Words of Jean-Paul Sartre," *Dissent* 27, no. 4 (Fall 1980):414–16.

16. See my article, "Sartre, the Algerian War, and *Les Séquestrés d'Altona,"* *Papers in Romance* 3, no. 2 (1981):81–90.

17. For details on this relationship, see Madsen, *Hearts and Minds,* pp. 194, 206.

18. *Œuvres romanesques,* p. lxxx ff; *TCF,* passim; *SV,* passim; *C,* passim; Octavio Paz, "Sartre in Our Time," *Dissent* 27, no. 4 (Fall 1980):427.

19. The manifesto called on Frenchmen to refuse to bear arms against the Algerian rebels. It is plain that his position *did* grant him some immunity, for he was never prosecuted; it was better for the government to ignore him than to create further controversy and ill will by making him a martyr.

20. Paz, "Sartre in Our Time," p. 427; *C,* 146, 148; *Œuvres romanesques,* p. ciii.

21. Arnold and Piriou, *Genèse et critique,* p. 29.

Chapter Two

1. Heidegger tries to dissociate himself from the existentialists, insisting that general being, not specific individual existences, interests him. Many points of contact remain, however. For his judgment on Sartre, see Roger Van Hecke's interview with him, *Figaro Littéraire,* 4 November 1950, p. 4. For a recent scholarly evaluation of the similarities in their ontology, see Charles E. Scott, "The Role of Ontology in Sartre and Heidegger," in Paul A. Schilpp, ed., *The Philosophy of Jean-Paul Sartre* (La Salle, Ill., 1981).

2. Jean-Paul Sartre, *The Transcendence of the Ego,* trans. F. Williams and R. Kirkpatrick (New York: Octagon Books, 1972), p. 35.

3. See Lévy, "Last Words," p. 398, for Sartre's comments on Kierkegaard's influence, which he recognized, although denying he knew anguish; see also *S* IX.

4. Douglas Collins, *Sartre as Biographer* (Cambridge, 1980), pp. 9–11.

5. Peter Caws, *Sartre* (London, 1979), p. 31. See also *WS,* 57.

6. See his article, "Une Idée fondamentale de la 'phénoménologie' de Husserl, l'intentionnalité," *Nouvelle Revue Française* 52 (January 1939):129–32, reprinted in *S* I.

7. Jean-Paul Sartre, *Imagination,* trans. Forrest Williams (Ann Arbor: University of Michigan Press, 1962), pp. 39, 131.

8. Jean-Paul Sartre, *The Emotions: Outline of a Theory,* trans. Bernard Frechtman (New York: Philosophical Library, 1948), pp. 53–57.

9. *The Transcendence of the Ego,* pp. 40–42, 44–45.

10. Sartre's reading may be erroneous. See Caws, *Sartre,* p. 52.

11. See *The Transcendence of the Ego,* introduction, p. 21. For a critique of this view, see Caws, *Sartre,* chapter 4.

12. See Caws, *Sartre,* p. 59.

13. *The Transcendence of the Ego,* pp. 23–24; also *BN,* 271–72.

14. Jean-Paul Sartre, *Psychology of the Imagination,* trans. B. Frechtman (New York: Philosophical Library, 1948), p. 268.

15. The following is chiefly an exposition rather than a critique. For a more synthetic and critical approach, see studies by Caws, Danto, and others listed in Alden and Brooks (see note on secondary sources under Bibliography). Page numbers in parentheses refer to the published translation; however, some of the translated terms and titles are my own version. I have used Sartre's capitalization.

16. Sartre sometimes capitalizes these terms, sometimes not. Since it is beyond the scope of this study to distinguish between his uses of them, small letters are used throughout.

17. He admits (*BN,* 76) that the term in-itself, already in use before he adopted it, is improper, because it implies a self, and self implies duality (it/itself); there is *total* identity in being-in-itself.

18. Cf. André Malraux's statement, "Every man dreams of being God," and the ensuing discussion in *La Condition humaine,* translated as *Man's Fate,* trans. Haakon M. Chevalier (New York: Modern Library, 1961), p. 228.

19. See *W,* 55–56, 158 on the attention paid to his body when he was small; see note 4, chapter 1, on his ugliness.

20. Sartre does not consider the obvious problem of animal sexuality, or that of animal consciousness in general.

21. Cf. Gaston Bachelard's analyses in *L'Eau et les rêves,* which Sartre mentions, and numerous literary works, e.g. Claudel's "L'Esprit et l'eau."

Chapter Three

1. See *WS,* 51–56, for information on the composition and reception of the work. See also François H. Lapointe, "A Selective Bibliography with Notations on Sartre's *Nausea* (1938–1980)," supplement to *Philosophy Today* 34 (Fall 1980):285–96.

2. However, readers have noted that the change of title obscures somewhat the artistic preoccupations of the hero. See George Howard Bauer, *Sartre and the Artist* (Chicago: University of Chicago Press, 1969), p. 43.

3. Roquentin as a common noun means someone who has aged. Sartre may have borrowed the name from Flaubert (*WS*, 55).

4. Jean-Paul Sartre, *Nausea,* trans. Lloyd Alexander (New York: New Directions, 1964), p. 18. This translation contains many errors, some of considerable importance.

5. In a number of respects, these mechanical bourgeois, invaded by their facticity, recall those of Proust (such as Legrandin) and anticipate those of Sarraute and Ionesco.

6. On portrait painting, see Jean-Paul Sartre, *Visages* (Paris: Seghers [1948]), "Portraits officiels." On art objects in *La Nausée,* see Bauer, *Sartre and the Artist,* pp. 13–44.

7. See *PL,* 121, for the origin of this revery.

8. The French text contains a number of verbal confusions (boue/boule, doigt/droit) which contribute to the meaning.

9. Unlike Alain Robbe-Grillet in *Pour un nouveau roman,* Sartre, while condemning anthropomorphism by implication, does not insist that the artist remove all humanizing metaphor from his language. Indeed, Sartre's is full of it.

10. This phrase, untranslated in the English version, is found in the original text of *La Nausée* in *Œuvres romanesques,* p. 159.

11. See Helmut Thielicke, "The Borderline Situation," in Joseph J. Kockelmans, ed., *Contemporary European Ethics* (Garden City, N.Y.: Doubleday, 1972), and *TS,* 20–21, 241.

12. Jean-Paul Sartre, *The Wall,* trans. Lloyd Alexander (New York: New Directions, 1948), pp. 9, 13.

13. Sweetness is the taste correlative of viscosity; see *BN,* 609.

14. One cannot but recall the symbolic sexual value assigned to the gun and knife by Freud. Sartre was doubtless familiar with Breton's definition of the supreme surrealist act: going into the street and firing at random into the crowd.

15. E.g., in Mauriac's *Thérèse Desqueyroux,* the heroine's reactions on her honeymoon. See *W,* 6.

Chapter Four

1. Jean-Paul Sartre, *What Is Literature?* trans. Bernard Frechtman (New York: Philosophical Library, 1949), pp. 224–29, 238–39. (Translated from "Qu'est-ce que la littérature?" *S* II.)

2. On praxis, see chapter 7.

3. For circumstances of composition and publication and Sartre's intentions, see *WS,* 112–15.

4. The name suggests "the man in the street."

5. Jean-Paul Sartre, *The Age of Reason,* trans. Eric Sutton (New York: Vintage, 1973), pp. 48, 52.

6. This gesture, which recalls Roquentin's, is foreshadowed when Boris plays with his alienated hand as if it were a pancake (p. 35). Konrad Bieber points out the resemblance between the gesture and that of one of Beauvoir's characters in *L'Invitée* (*She Came to Stay*) and suggests Nietzsche as a model. See his *Simone de Beauvoir* (Boston, 1979), p. 158. But the example of Tchen in Malraux's *La Condition humaine,* with its metaphysical overtones, may have been more crucial.

7. See *WS,* 112–16 for information on the composition of the novel and Sartre's intentions.

8. Jean-Paul Sartre, *The Reprieve,* trans. Eric Sutton (New York: Knopf, 1947), p. 326.

9. See Francis L. Loewenheim, *Peace or Appeasement? Hitler, Chamberlain, and the Munich Crisis* (Boston: Houghton Mifflin, 1965).

10. The loading of the invalids into freight cars foreshadows what the Germans did with French prisoners and deportees.

11. The parallel is supported by Sartre's comments in *Baudelaire,* trans. Martin Turnell (New York: New Directions, 1947), p. 60.

12. *What is Literature?* p. 76. For other remarks on Jews, see *WS,* 143 ff., 466; Lévy, "Last Words," pp. 417–21; and Jean-Paul Sartre, *Réflexions sur la question juive* (Paris: Gallimard, 1954), trans. as *Anti-Semite and Jew* (New York: Schocken, 1948).

13. A phrase repeatedly used concerning the defeated men.

14. Jean-Paul Sartre, *Troubled Sleep,* trans. Gerard Hopkins (New York: Knopf, 1951), p. 96.

15. The passage in which wounded Frenchmen in the burning town hall scream in agony and are shot at by those in the tower recalls the attack on the police station in *La Condition humaine* and Tchen's similar strong sympathy with the sufferers.

16. See Jean-Paul Sartre, "Le Cas Nizan," *Les Temps Modernes,* no. 22 (July 1947), pp. 181–84, and his preface to Nizan's *Aden Arabie,* in *S* IV, 130–88. But Brunet in the earlier volumes also resembles Nizan somewhat. Michel Contat points out that Schneider is something of a blend of Nizan and Sartre, that is, a Communist party member who nevertheless is critical of the party, who is both a partisan and a solitary intellectual. Nizan was killed in 1940; Sartre kept his friend alive by literary creation. See *Œuvres romanesques,* p. 2107.

17. Jean-Paul Sartre, "Drôle d'amitié," *Les Temps Modernes,* nos. 49, 50 (November, December 1949), pp. 769–806, 1009–39. Beauvoir gives in *FC,* 194–95, a summary of how Sartre planned to finish the story. It is also included in *WS,* 233–34, and *Œuvres romanesques,* pp. 2104–5. Some important unpublished portions are now included in the latter, p. 1585 ff. The story is both dramatically and ideologically interesting.

18. Richard Crossman wrote that "the true ex-Communist can never again be a whole personality." See introduction to his *The God That Failed* (New York: Harper's, 1949), p. 11.

19. For a discussion of freedom in these novels, see Catharine Savage, *Malraux, Sartre, and Aragon As Political Novelists* (Gainesville: University of Florida Press, 1964).

Chapter Five

1. For information about Sartre's early dramatic attempts, some dating from secondary school days, see *TS*, 12–13.

2. Sartre ceased writing apparently because he was convinced the time for *individual* theatrical efforts was past; only collective undertakings were suitable. See *TS*, 11; *C*, 243.

3. See chapter 3 supra and *TS*, 21, 241.

4. See *TS*, 57–59, and Jean-Paul Sartre, "Beyond Bourgeois Theatre," *Tulane Drama Review* 5, no. 3 (March 1961):3–11.

5. This approach makes Sartre a forerunner of the theater of the absurd. See *TS*, 190.

6. Northrop Frye has identified in modern literature a movement from low-mimetic (bourgeois) and then ironic, back to mythic. See his *Anatomy of Criticism* (Princeton: Princeton University Press, 1957), pp. 33–42.

7. The expression denotes plays appealing to large audiences.

8. *Bariona* will not be discussed, since it was published only recently, in special circumstances, and Sartre considered it very poor (*C*, 237). See *WS*, 412–13, and vol. II of the same work; *TS*, 219–21; Desautels, "Sartre of Stalag 12D," 201–6.

9. For an examination of classical sources and modern parallels, see the edition of F. C. St. Aubyn and R. G. Marshall (New York: Harper and Row, 1963), and their bibliography. For other facts on the play, see *WS*, 84–89.

10. There is also an allusion to Pascal's famous passage on man in comparison to the universe.

11. For this judgment and other information, see *WS*, 134–36.

12. Beauvoir calls it "individualistic pride" in contrast to Canoris, the effective militant, whom Sartre prefers (*FC*, 112).

13. For a survey of the reactions as well as information on the composition and productions, see *WS*, 137–40.

14. Other titles have been used for English translations, such as *Crime passionnel,* and *Red Gloves* for the 1948 New York production. See *WS*, 189–91, and *TS*, 95 for information on the play and erroneous interpretations.

15. For an analysis of it, see *WS*, 603.

16. Jean-Paul Sartre, *No Exit and Three Other Plays,* trans. S. Gilbert and L. Abel (New York: Vintage, 1955), p. 136.

17. For Sartre's comments on the play cited in this paragraph, see *WS*, 186–93, and *TS*, 246–47.

18. A list and analyses of all his films can be found in *WS*, 162–64, 194–96, 326–27, 601–12, 617.

19. See introduction to Mary E. Storer's edition (New York: Appleton-Century-Crofts, 1952); she calls the main characters "faithful exponents of Sartrean philosophy" (p. xxiv).

20. Sartre was criticizing all imperialism, Soviet and American. He said he did not mean to justify all opportunistic politics, e.g., Stalin's. See *WS*, 193–94, and *TS*, 367–70.

Chapter Six

1. Similarly, Orestes' father is dead, and Hugo tries to deny his father. Jeanson finds that bastard, impostor, and traitor are all related and all stand for the intellectual, i.e., Sartre himself (*SV*, 211–12). Sartre later agreed that all intellectuals were bastards, in the positive sense. See his interview with Pierre Verstraeten, "Jean-Paul Sartre: 'Je ne suis plus réaliste,'" *Gulliver*, no. 1 (November 1972), pp. 38–47.

2. "I became a traitor and have remained one" (*W*, 149). I have discussed this theme elsewhere; see infra, note 15.

3. See *WS*, 246–56, and *TS*, 268–81, for details on the play's composition, presentation, reception, and sources.

4. A parallel with *Le Soulier de satin* has been noted (*WS*, 255).

5. For parallels with Marlowe's *Doctor Faustus,* see Dorothy McCall, *The Theatre of Jean-Paul Sartre* (New York: Columbia University Press, 1969), p. 28.

6. Jean-Paul Sartre, *The Devil and the Good Lord, and Two Other Plays,* trans. Kitty Black and S. and G. Leeson (New York: Knopf, 1960), p. 73.

7. This foreshadows Sartre's statements on the uselessness and failure of nonviolence in a world based on violence. See *S V*, 167–93, and Lévy, "Last Words," pp. 414–17; see also Sartre's preface to Michèle Manceaux, *Les Maos en France* (Paris: Gallimard, 1972), p. 7.

8. Sartre later criticized this elitist conclusion, as a "reflex of the classic intellectual," saying that Goetz should have remained a simple soldier. See Verstraeten, "Jean-Paul Sartre," p. 39.

9. See *WS*, 287–92, and *TS*, 282–91, for details on this and other aspects of the play's history; also Robert Lorris, *Sartre dramaturge* (Paris: Nizet, 1975), p. 290.

10. For comparisons between the Dumas and Sartre texts, see Robert J. Nelson, "Sartre: The Play as Lie," in his *Play Within a Play: The Dramatist's Conception of His Art* (New Haven: Yale University Press, 1958), pp. 100–114.

11. *The Devil and the Good Lord and Two Other Plays,* p. 171.

12. Sartre reintroduces the theme, again using the example of Kean, in *L'Idiot de la famille;* see *TS,* 195–207.

13. McCall, *Theatre of Jean-Paul Sartre,* p. 99.

14. Nelson, "Sartre: The Play as Lie," pp. 107–8.

15. For a discussion of the ending and a general thematic analysis of the play, see my article, "Sartre's *Kean* and Self-Portrait," *French Review* 55, special issue no. 7 (1982), 109–22.

16. See *WS,* 305–11, and *TS,* 292–98, for details on sources, performances, reception, and Sartre's comments.

17. He can be compared to Genet (see chapter 7 infra), who similarly needs private property in order to live by theft.

18. McCall, *Theatre of Jean-Paul Sartre,* pp. 93, 97.

19. See *WS,* 355 ff., and *TS,* 299–359, and Oreste F. Pucciani, "An Interview with Jean-Paul Sartre," *Tulane Drama Review* 5, no. 3 (March 1961):13. See also my article, "Sartre, the Algerian War, and *Les Séquestrés d'Altona.*"

20. Pucciani, "Interview," pp. 12–13, 18. See, however, *C,* 217.

21. See *TS,* 333–36.

22. Jean-Paul Sartre, "Beyond Bourgeois Theatre," pp. 3–5.

23. Pucciani, "Interview," p. 16; *TS,* 355.

24. See Victor Brombert, *The Romantic Prison: The French Tradition* (Princeton: Princeton University Press, 1978).

25. See *TS,* 356, and Marie-Denise Boros, *Un Séquestré: l'homme sartrien* (Paris: Nizet, 1968).

26. Sartre stressed the importance of their Protestantism. See *TS,* 323–25, 341–42.

27. It has been noted that the name may stand for France itself. See Jean-Paul Sartre, *The Condemned of Altona,* trans. S. and G. Leeson (New York: Vintage, 1963), p. xi.

28. On the crab motif, see chapter 1 supra, *TS,* 155, and Marie-Denise Boros, "La Métaphore du crabe dans l'œuvre littéraire de Jean-Paul Sartre," *PMLA* 81, no. 5 (October 1966):446–50.

29. Pucciani, "Interview," p. 14. Similarly, Jacques Lacan points out in *Ecrits* (Paris: Seuil, 1966) that altruism is always the product of a wish to destroy (p. 100).

30. Sartre's own interpretation of the Johanna-Frantz relationship, stressing Johanna's need for him to affirm her beauty, can be found in *TS,* 319–22.

31. See *WS,* 356.

32. Arnold and Piriou, *Genèse et critique,* pp. 9–10, 37.

33. Albert Camus, *The Fall* (New York: Vintage, 1956), p. 55.

34. Jean-Paul Sartre, *The Trojan Women,* adapted by Ronald Duncan (New York: Knopf, 1967), p. xii. Other information about Sartre's aims can be found here and in *TS,* 360–66.

35. *Les Troyennes* can be compared to Jean Giraudoux's *La Guerre de Troie n'aura pas lieu (Tiger at the Gates)*, which, while condemning war, suggests that it is unavoidable and exerts a powerful appeal.

Chapter Seven

1. He occasionally had plans for plays and novels but did not carry them out. See, e.g., *S* X, 187.

2. See Benjamin Suhl, *Sartre: The Philosopher As Literary Critic* (New York: Columbia University Press, 1970); Michel Sicard, *La Critique littéraire de Jean-Paul Sartre*, vol. 1: *Objets et thèmes* (Paris, 1976); Christina Howells, *Sartre's Theory of Literature* (London, 1979).

3. Jean-Paul Sartre, *Literary and Philosophic Essays*, trans. Annette Michelson (New York: Collier Books, 1962), p. 25. This volume contains translations of several important essays.

4. For a short critical appraisal of the Husserl article, see Arnold and Piriou, *Genèse et critique*, p. 5.

5. Cf. *TS*, 158–59. One wonders what Sartre's reaction would be to the conservative stance of an artist such as T. S. Eliot.

6. Pucciani, "Interview," p. 12; *S* IX, 25, 38.

7. It should be added that, in any case, virtually no criticism can "explain" poetry, either its origin or its effects.

8. For Sartre's views on Freud, see *S* IX, 103–8.

9. Jean-Paul Sartre, *Saint Genet, comédien et martyr* (Paris: Gallimard, 1952), p. 536. This has been translated as *Saint Genet, Actor and Martyr*, trans. Bernard Frechtman (New York: Braziller, 1963). Translations here are my own.

10. Douglas Collins has analyzed (pp. 80–110) the dialectical method used by Sartre in his portrait of Genet and the particular influence of Hegel, Marx, and others.

11. But Sartre later judged that the study was inadequate, since the conditioning of Genet by the events of his objective history and the role of the specific twentieth-century milieu are not indicated (*S* IX, 114).

12. Quoted by Arnold and Piriou, *Genèse et critique*, p. 5.

13. Marc Bensimon, "D'un mythe à l'autre: essai sur *Les Mots*," *Revue des Sciences Humaines*, no. 119 (1965), p. 416.

14. See *WS*, 430, on his attenuation of his original harshness.

15. Bensimon, "D'un mythe à l'autre," pp. 422–24.

16. William L. Howarth, "Some Principles of Autobiography," *New Literary History* 5, no. 2 (Winter 1974):363–81.

17. Bensimon, "D'un mythe à l'autre," p. 416.

18. Similarly, he has been unable to explain why some bourgeois intellectuals are critical of their society and others not. See Verstraeten, "Jean-Paul Sartre," pp. 40–41. In contrast to this interpretation, Sartre at the end of his life

acknowledged candidly to Beauvoir that, as a teenager and later, he thought himself both extremely intelligent and a genius (though these are not quite the same), and it seems that he considered these capacities inborn. See *C,* 185–89, 210–11.

19. E.g., the opinion of P.-H. Simon. See Bensimon, "D'un mythe à l'autre," pp. 415–16.

20. Robert Champigny, "Trying to Understand *L'Idiot,*" *Diacritics* 2, no. 2 (Summer 1972):2–3.

21. See below, the next section of this chapter.

22. Max Charlesworth, *The Existentialists and Jean-Paul Sartre* (New York, 1976), p. 117.

23. Graham Good, "Sartre's Flaubert, Flaubert's Sartre," *Novel* 7, no. 2 (Winter 1974):181.

24. Portions of the second volume were published in the *New Left Review,* no. 100 (November 1976–January 1977). The entire manuscript is analyzed in Ronald Aronson, *Jean-Paul Sartre–Philosophy in the World* (London, 1980), pp. 272–86.

25. *CRD,* 153; "L'Anthropologie" in *S* IX, 83–98.

26. References and quotations come from the French version of *CRD,* in my translation. Though a good English translation exists (see bibliography), the introductory section, published earlier, is omitted, and the translations are on occasion somewhat free; the translator has even reorganized the text somewhat. A table of comparative pagination in the translated version allows one to utilize both texts with ease.

27. Wilfrid Desan, "An English Version of Sartre's Main Philosophical Work," *Philosophy Today* 24, no. 3–4 (Fall 1980):269.

28. Arthur Lessing, "Marxist Existentialism," *Review of Metaphysics* 20, no. 3 (March 1967):473.

29. Lessing, "Marxist Existentialism," p. 472.

30. Desan, "English Version," pp. 265–66.

31. See *S* IX, 40, 78; *CRD,* 306, 316, 320.

32. Desan, "English Version," p. 269; *SV,* 212. See also chapter 6, notes 2, 15.

Chapter Eight

1. Paz, "Sartre in Our Time," p. 428.

Selected Bibliography

PRIMARY SOURCES

Sartre's bibliography is enormous. For works prior to 1974, most of which will not be listed here (but, if referred to in the text, are given in the notes), consult the indispensable study by Michel Contat and Michel Rybalka, *The Writings of Jean-Paul Sartre,* vol. 1, *A Bibliographical Life* (abbreviated *WS*) and vol. 2, *Selected Prose* (Evanston: Northwestern University Press, 1974), translated by Richard C. McCleary from the one-volume French edition, *Les Ecrits de Sartre* (Paris: Gallimard, 1970). The translated version is up to date through 1973. Works published since 1973 are given below, as are all others by Sartre which are designated by abbreviations in this study.

Being and Nothingness: An Essay on Phenomenological Ontology. Translated by Hazel E. Barnes. New York: Philosophical Library, 1956.

Between Existentialism and Marxism. Translated by John Matthews. New York: Morrow, 1974.

Critique of Dialectical Reason. Translated by Alan Sheridan-Smith. London: NLB, 1976.

The Family Idiot. Translated by Carol Cosman. Vol. 1. Chicago: University of Chicago Press, 1981.

Life/Situations: Essays Written and Spoken. Translated by Paul Auster and Lydia Davis. New York: Pantheon Books, 1977. (Translation of *Situations* X.)

Œuvres romanesques. Edited by Michel Contat and Michel Rybalka. Paris: Gallimard, 1981.

On a raison de se révolter. In collaboration with Philippe Gavi and Pierre Victor. Paris: Gallimard, 1974.

Sartre. (Text of film "Sartre par lui-même.") Paris: Gallimard, 1977.

Sartre by Himself. Translated by Richard Seaver. New York: Urizen Books, 1978. (Translation of *Sartre.*)

Sartre: images d'une vie. Commentaries by Simone de Beauvoir. Paris: Gallimard, 1978. (Iconography.)

Sartre on Theatre. Edited by Michel Contat and Michel Rybalka. Translated by Frank Jellinek. New York: Pantheon Books, 1976. (Translation of *Un Théâtre de situations.*)

Situations I–X. Paris: Gallimard, 1947–1976.

Un Théâtre de situations. Edited by Michel Contat and Michel Rybalka. Paris: Gallimard, 1973.

SECONDARY SOURCES

A lengthy and authoritative annotated bibliography of books and essays on Sartre, arranged topically, can be found in Douglas W. Alden and Richard A. Brooks, *A Critical Bibliography of French Literature,* vol. 6: *The Twentieth Century,* 3 vols. (Syracuse: Syracuse University Press, 1980). Because this indispensable tool includes virtually everything of importance published before 1975, such works will not generally be listed here; they are, however, given in the notes if referred to in the text. The following list includes volumes from 1975 on and works on Sartre designated by abbreviations in this study.

1. Bibliography

Lapointe, François L. "A Selective Bibliography with Notations on Sartre's *Nausea* (1938–1980)." Supplement to *Philosophy Today* 24, no. 3–4 (Fall 1980):285–96. Very useful; annotated.

———, and Lapointe, Claire. "A Bibliography of Jean-Paul Sartre, 1970–1975: The Anglo-American Response to Jean-Paul Sartre." *Philosophy Today* 19, no. 4 (Winter 1975):341–57. Not annotated. Lists eighteen books, plus doctoral dissertations and articles, arranged topically.

———. *Jean-Paul Sartre and His Critics.* 2d ed. Bowling Green, Ohio: Philosophy Documentation Center, 1980. See comments on previous edition in Alden and Brooks.

Wilcocks, Robert. *Jean-Paul Sartre: A Bibliography of International Criticism.* Edmonton: University of Alberta Press, 1975.

2. Books

Adloff, Jean Gabriel. *Sartre; index du Corpus philosophique.* Vol. 1: *"L'Etre et le néant," "Critique de la raison dialectique."* Paris: Klincksieck, 1981. Useful tool enabling one to find references and passages in these two works. Alphabetical listing of names, philosophical terms, topics.

Anderson, Thomas. *The Foundations and Structure of Sartrean Ethics.* Lawrence: The Regents Press of Kansas, 1979. Lucid exposition of Sartre's moral theory, its foundations in ontology, and its political implications. *CRD* featured.

Aron, Raymond. *History and the Dialectic of Violence: An Analysis of Sartre's "Critique de la raison dialectique."* Translated by Barry Cooper. New York: Harper and Row, 1975. By a former friend of Sartre; analyzes the political implications of *CRD.*

Aronson, Ronald. *Jean-Paul Sartre–Philosophy in the World.* London: NLB, 1980. Chronological study of the development of Sartre's thought, in a Marxist framework, especially of its concern for freedom and his use of ideas and literature as political tools. Well written.

Autour de Jean-Paul Sartre: Littérature et philosophie. Introduction de Pierre Verstraeten. Paris: Gallimard, 1982. Important discussion and general view of Sartre, concentrating on major themes.

Barnes, Hazel E. *Sartre and Flaubert.* Chicago:. University of Chicago Press, 1982.

Beauvoir, Simone de. *All Said and Done.* Translated by Patrick O'Brien. New York: Putnam, 1974. Translation of *Tout Compte fait* (1972), which completes her memoirs.

————. *La Cérémonie des adieux, suivi de Entretiens avec Jean-Paul Sartre.* Paris: Gallimard, 1981. Recounts the last ten years of their shared life. Long interviews.

————. *The Force of Circumstance.* Translated by Richard Howard. New York: Putnam's, 1964. Her life and Sartre's from the Liberation to Algerian independence.

————. *Memoirs of a Dutiful Daughter.* Translated by James Kirkup. New York: Harper and Row, 1974. Recounts her meeting with Sartre at the university.

————. *The Prime of Life.* Translated by Peter Green. New York: World Publishing Co., 1962. Beauvoir's and Sartre's activities in the 1930s and during the war.

Bieber, Konrad. *Simone de Beauvoir.* Boston: Twayne, 1979. Many references to Sartre in the index; some attempt to assess their relationships and his influence on her.

Brombert, Victor. *The Romantic Prison: The French Tradition.* Studies literal and figurative imprisonment and entrapment in Sartre's theater and fiction.

Burnier, Michel-Antoine. *Le Testament de Sartre.* Paris: Olivier Orban, 1982.

Cagnon, Maurice, ed. *Ethique et esthétique dans la littérature française du XXᵉ siècle.* Saratoga, Calif.: Anma Libri, 1978. Contains two excellent essays on Sartre, one on *La Nausée* (D. O'Connell), the other on *Les Mains sales* (M. Issacharoff).

Carson, Ronald A. *Jean-Paul Sartre.* Valley Forge, Pa.: Judson Press, 1974.

Catalano, Joseph S. *A Commentary on Jean-Paul Sartre's "Being and Nothingness."* New York: Harper and Row, 1974. Summary and explanation of *BN,* for novices.

Caws, Peter. *Sartre.* London: Routledge and Kegan Paul, 1979. The best available analysis and commentary on Sartre's philosophy. Assumes considerable prior knowledge.

Champigny, Robert. *Sartre and Drama.* Columbia, S.C.: French Literature Publications, 1982.

Charlesworth, Max. *The Existentialists and Jean-Paul Sartre.* New York: St. Martin's, 1976. Excellent overview, with up-to-date critical opinions. Lengthy interviews with Sartre in English.

Chiodi, Pietro. *Sartre and Marxism.* Translated by Kate Soper. London: Harvester Press, 1976. Deals with *CRD.* See comments on the 1965 Italian version in Alden and Brooks.

Collins, Douglas. *Sartre as Biographer.* Cambridge: Harvard University Press, 1980. Excellent study of the biographies.

Colombel, Jeannette. *Sartre ou le parti de vivre.* Paris: Grasset, 1981. Chiefly on political and philosophic works. Based on interviews.

Craib, Ian. *Existentialism and Sociology: A Study of Jean-Paul Sartre.* Cambridge: Cambridge University Press, 1976. Argues that Sartre occupies a central position in modern Marxist thought and is an important sociologist.

Danto, Arthur. *Jean-Paul Sartre.* New York: Viking, 1975. Useful analysis of Sartre's philosophy, chiefly *BN.*

L'Esprit Créateur. Issue on Sartre, 17, no. 1 (Spring 1977). Articles on odors and surrealistic elements in *La Nausée;* mirrors in his works; *Le Mur;* interviews as autobiography; his views on surrealism, poetry, politics and *négritude.*

Fell, Joseph P. *Heidegger and Sartre.* New York: Columbia University Press, 1979.

French Review. Vol. 55, special issue no. 7, "Sartre and Biography." Essays on *Les Mots, Les Chemins de la liberté,* Beauvoir as a biographer of Sartre, etc. Recent biography and bibliography.

George, François. *Deux Etudes sur Sartre.* Paris: Christian Bourgois, 1976. Somewhat rambling discussions of Sartre's philosophic ideas. Requires close acquaintance with texts.

Hayim, Gila J. *The Existential Sociology of Jean-Paul Sartre.* Amherst: University of Massachusetts Press, 1980. Treatment of both *BN* and *CRD* in relation to sociological perspectives and topics. Considers influence of Hegel and Marx.

Helbo, André. *L'Enjeu du discours: lecture de Sartre.* Paris: Editions Complexe, 1978. Semiotic approach to Sartre.

Hodard, Philippe. *Sartre entre Marx et Freud.* Paris: J.-P. Delarge, 1979. Concentrates on ties between *BN* and *CRD;* good evaluation of his Marxism.

Hollier, Denis. *Politique de la prose: Jean-Paul Sartre et l'année quarante.* Paris: Gallimard, 1982.

Howells, Christina. *Sartre's Theory of Literature.* London: Modern Humanities Research Association, 1979. Learned, philosophical study of Sartre's understanding of imagination and language; examination of his criticism.

Issacharoff, Michael, and **Vilquin, Jean-Claude,** eds. *Sartre et la mise en signe.* Lexington, Ky.: French Forum Monographs, 1982.

Jeanson, Francis. *Sartre dans sa vie.* Paris: Seuil, 1974. The best biography yet, by someone who knew him well. Many interesting quotations. Photographs but no index.

————. *Sartre and the Problem of Morality.* Translated by Robert V. Stone. Bloomington: Indiana University Press, 1980. Translation of the 1947 and 1965 French version, still important. Excellent introduction, which summarizes Jeanson's ideas and evolution of Sartre's ethical thought.

Kellman, Steven G. *The Self-Begetting Novel.* New York: Columbia University Press, 1980. Chapter on *La Nausée.*

Kirsner, Douglas. *The Schizoid World of Jean-Paul Sartre and R. D. Laing.* St. Lucia: University of Queensland Press, 1976. Philosophic study of Sartre and his themes, using his own biographic method, which relates him to his time.

LaCapra, Dominick. *A Preface to Sartre.* Ithaca: Cornell University Press, 1978. A deconstructive reading.

Laraque, Franck. *La Révolte dans le théâtre de Sartre vu par un homme du Tiers Monde.* Paris: Jean-Pierre Delarge, 1976. A nontechnical study, concentrating on politics.

Lawler, James. *The Existentialist Marxism of Jean-Paul Sartre.* Amsterdam: Grüner, 1976. Study of Sartre's philosophic texts compared to Marx, Engels, etc. Concludes that existentialism is essentially non-Marxist.

Madsen, Axel. *Hearts and Minds: The Common Journey of Jean-Paul Sartre and Simone de Beauvoir.* New York: Morrow, 1977. Biography, based on their writings and interviews with Sartre. Very readable. Iconography and index.

Mészáros, István. *The Work of Sartre.* Vol. 1: *Search for Freedom.* Atlantic Highlands, N.J.: Humanities Press, 1980. Provides a good survey of his development from a philosophic point of view and then an analysis of the early works, stressing the concept of freedom.

Morris, Phyllis Sutton. *Sartre's Concept of a Person: An Analytic Approach.* Amherst: University of Massachusetts Press, 1976. Topic approached partly from the point of view of analytic philosophy. Deals with the identity of persons, the existence of others, and moral agents.

Nuttall, A. D. *A Common Sky: Philosophy and the Literary Imagination.* Berkeley: University of California Press, 1974. Excellent pages on *La Nausée,* e.g., on solipsism.

Obliques. Special issue on Sartre, nos. 18–19 (1979). Contains interviews, important fragment on Mallarmé, additions to bibliography in *WS,* pages on ethics, etc.

Pacaly, Josette. *Sartre au miroir: Une Lecture psychanalytique de ses écrits biographiques.* Paris: Klincksieck, 1980. Concludes he was highly neurotic, had a castration complex, and did not relate well to others.

Papers in Romance. Special issue on Sartre, 3, no. 2 (Spring 1981). Treats Sartre and films, painting, Montaigne, etc.

Philosophy Today. 19, no. 4 (Winter 1975). Eight articles on Sartre and related topics, e.g. totalization.

Philosophy Today. Special issue on Sartre, 24, no. 3–4 (Fall 1980). Articles on bad faith, the self and others, phenomenology and Marxism, *CRD,* and books on Sartre.

Plank, William. *Sartre and Surrealism.* Ann Arbor: UMI Research Press, 1981.

Poster, Mark. *Existential Marxism in Postwar France.* Princeton: Princeton University Press, 1975.

Ranwez, Alain D. *Jean-Paul Sartre's "Les Temps Modernes": A Literary History, 1945–52.* Troy, N.Y.: Whitston Publishing Co., 1981. Survey of fiction and articles appearing in *TM;* assessment of major trends. Indexes.

Schilpp, Paul A., ed. *The Philosophy of Jean-Paul Sartre.* La Salle, Ill.: Open Court Publishing Co., 1981. Extremely important collection of essays. Interview and bibliography.

Schwarz, Theodor. *J.-P. Sartre et le marxisme.* Translated by Marc Reinhardt. Lausanne: L'Age d'Homme, 1977. Introduction on Sartre's derivation from Heidegger and his existentialism; analysis of major points of *CRD.*

Sicard, Michel. *La Critique littéraire de Jean-Paul Sartre.* Vol. 1: *Objets et thèmes.* Paris: Minard, 1976. Treats Sartre's critical works as a whole. Emphasis is linguistic, thematic, and psychoanalytic. Shows ties to other works.

Silverman, Hugh, and Elliston, Frederick, eds. *Jean-Paul Sartre: Contemporary Approaches to His Philosophy.* Pittsburgh: Duquesne University Press, 1980. Extremely useful collection of important essays, all in English here. Treats such topics as bad faith, the body, the self, influences. List of all Sartre's works available in English.

Stack, George. *Sartre's Philosophy of Social Existence.* St. Louis: Green, 1977.

Todd, Olivier. *Un Fils rebelle.* Paris: Grasset, 1981. Very critical evaluation by the husband of Nizan's daughter.

Verona, Luciano. *Le Théâtre de Jean-Paul Sartre.* Milan: Cisalpino-Goliardica, 1979. Plot summaries; documentation not up-to-date. Politics treated from a socialist viewpoint.

Index

Abraham (in Old Testament), 37
Absurdity, 46, 51
Afghanistan, 16
Agrégation, 6
Alain. *See* Chartier, Emile
Alcan, Félix (publisher), 21
Algeria, 12, 103; war in, 14, 15, 94, 97, 98
Alienation, 12, 31, 110–11, 116, 119
Alleg, Henri: *La Question,* 14
American novelists, 55, 101
Analysis, 112–13, 117
Analytical reason. *See* Analysis
Anguish, 21, 27–28, 37
Anouilh, Jean, 90, 94
Anthropology, 110, 112
Anthropomorphizing, 45
Anti-Semitism, 53. *See also* Jewish question; Jews
Anti-value, 36
Arab-Israeli war, 15
Aristotelian philosophy, 72, 101
Aristotle, 112
Aron, Raymond, 20
Art, 25, 35, 43, 46–47, 106
Atelier, L' (theater), 10
Atheism, 4, 38, 89, 120. *See also* Sartre, Jean-Paul, Religious views

Baader, Andreas, 16
Baader-Meinhof group, 16
Bachelard, Gaston: *L'Eau et les rêves,* 125n21
Bad faith, 23, *28,* 32, 37, 42, 43, 57, 63, 79, 83, 86, 105

Balzac, Honoré de: *Eugénie Grandet,* 46
Barrault, Jean-Louis, 86
Barthes, Roland, 94
Basque question, 15
Bastardy, 85, 91, 105, 129n1
Baudelaire, Charles, 3, 4, 64, *104– 105,* 106
Beauvoir, Simone de, *5–7,* 8, 9, 10, 11, 12, 14, 15, 16, 36, 39, 108; *Pour une morale de l'ambiguïté,* 36
Being, 20, 26–27, 29, 35, 53. *See also* Ontology
Belief, 28
Bergson, Henri, 5, 21, 29
Berkeley, George, 22
Beyle, Henri [pseud. Stendhal], 4, 6, 47
Bifur, 8
Binet, Alfred, 24
Blanchot, Maurice, 101
Bourgeoisie, 7, 10, 12, 13, 14, 33, 43, 44, 46, 52–54, 80, 85, 94, 102, 107, 109, ł10
Brasseur, Pierre, 80, 86, 90, 91
Brazil, 15
Brecht, Bertolt, 94, 98
Breton, André, 126n14
Bretons, 15
Butor, Michel: *L'Emploi du temps,* 40
By-itself, 27

Café de Flore, 10
Calvin, Jean, 120
Camus, Albert, 10, 11, 14, 31, 47, 73, 75, 102, 103, 104; *La Chute,*

98; *L'Etranger,* 101; *L'Homme ré-volté,* 14
Capitalism, 7, 10, 53, 95, 97, 119
Cartesianism, *18–19,* 22, 34, 112
Castro, Fidel, 15
Catholics, 37
Cause du Peuple, La, 16
Caws, Peter, 21
Cayrol, Jean, 9
Céline. *See* Destouches, Louis-Ferdinand
Central America, 12
Cervantes, Miguel de: *Don Quixote,* 2; *El Rufián dichoso,* 86
Chamberlain, Neville, 61, 62
Champigny, Robert, 109
Chaplin, Charles, 11
Chartier, Emile [pseud. Alain], 5, 21
Chateaubriand, François-René de, 16
Chestnut tree, 46, 62
China, 14
Cinema, 7. *See also* Films
Classless society, 113
Claudel, Paul, 7, 86; "L'Esprit et l'eau," 125n21
Coefficient of adversity, 34, 115
Cogito, *18–19,* 24, 26, 30, 37, 45, 52, 63
Cold War, 12, 85, 92–93
Collectivities, 113, 115, *116–17*
Colonialism, 98, 103
Combat (Resistance group and newspaper), 10, 11
Committed literature, 56, 94, 101–102
Communist Party, 8, 10, 11, 13, 14, 37, 63, 69, 82, 93, 103, 112
Complexes, 35
Conception, 25
Consciousness, *22–23,* 26–28, 114; in *L'Age de raison,* 58; always consciousness of something, 22; in *Les*

Chemins de la liberté, 70; and embodiment, 31–32; and emotion, 24; as free, 25, 27; in Husserl's thought, 19–20; image in, 21; and intentionality, 23; in "Le Mur," 49; in *La Nausée,* 41, 46; nonpositional, nonthetic, prereflexive or unreflexive quality, 22, 24, 26; and nothingness, 25, 27; and other consciousnesses, 31–32; positional, thetic, or reflexive quality, 22, 23, 24–25, 26; replaced by *le vécu,* 109; as self-awareness, 22; in *Le Sursis,* 61, 64–65; unity of, 28
Contat, Michel, 1, 16
Contingency, 6, 8, 26, *28–29,* 31, 36, 49
Corneille, Pierre: *Le Cid,* 80
Cornell University, 15
Courcy, Frédéric de, 90
Cowardice, 38, 64, 67
Cuba, 12, 15
Czechoslovakia, 16, 61, 62, 63, 65

Daladier, Edouard, 61, 62
Dante Alighieri, 76
Dasein, 26
De trop, 46. *See also* Contingency
Death, as possibility, 34
Desan, Wilfrid, 115
Descartes, René, *18–19,* 21, 29, 101
Despair, 37, 74–75. *See also* Anguish
Destouches, Louis Ferdinand [pseud. Céline], 7
Determinism, 13, 33, 104, 106, 114
Detotalized totality, 36, 61, 65, 113
Dialectical materialism, 99, 112, 113
Dialectical reason, 94, 95, 109–10, 113, 117
Dialectics, 105, 111, *112–13,* 116, 117, 120
Diderot, Denis, 92

Dos Passos, John, 7, 61, 101
Dostoyevsky, Feodor, 6, 37
Doubrovsky, Serge, 110
Drama, Sartre's understanding of, 72, 94–95
Dualism, 22, 23, 26, 31, 36, 105
Dullin, Charles, 10, 73
Dumas, Alexandre, the elder: *Kean*, 90, 91
Dürer, Albrecht, 39

Ego, *22–23*, 82, 91–92, 104
Egypt, 15
El Kaïm, Arlette, 15, 16
Embodiment, 26, 28, *31*, 40–41, 44–45, 49, 50, 51, 60
Emotion, 24
Engels, Friedrich, 114
England, 37, 66, 68, 91, 116
Enlightenment, 102
Epistemological quest, 40
Erostratus, 50
Essence, 37, 52, 53, 82. *See also* Being
Ethics, 13, 26, 27, 33, 36, 38, 65, 86, 89
Euripides, 99; *The Trojan Women*, 16, 98
Evil, 77, 87–89, 105–106
Existentialism, 11, 18, 20, *36–38*, 97, 106, 109, 111, 112

Facticity, *29–31, 34*, 40, 41, 50, 51, 57
Fanon, Frantz: *Les Damnés de la terre*, 103
Farigoule, Louis [pseud. Jules Romains], 56
Fascism, 7, 8, 14, 38, 53, 58, 69
Faulkner, William, 7, 101
Fictional theory, 55–56
Fifth Republic, 14
Films, 16, 80, *82–84*, 108

Flaubert, Achille, 109, 110
Flaubert, Gustave, 3, 16, 17, 101, *108–11*, 113, 117; *Madame Bovary*, 109
For-itself, *22*, 26, 28–29, 36, 40, 90, 91
For-others, *30–33*, 34, 40, 90, 91, 105
Free French, 37
Freedom, 23, 119, 120; in *L'Age de raison*, 58–59; in *CRD*, 114–16; in *Les Chemins de la liberté*, 56, 70; and choice, 33; "condemned to be free," 30, 59; consciousness as free, 25; in *Le Diable et le Bon Dieu*, 89; in drama, 72, 85; and facticity, 34; as foundation of values, 37; limited by conditions or alienated, 12–13, 106, 111, 119; and literature, 102; meaning in wartime, 9–10; in *La Mort dans l'âme*, 67; in *Les Mouches*, 73–74; in *La Nausée*, 46; not identical to power, 33; and nothingness, 27; ontological and political freedom, 37–38; and relations with others, 32; in *Le Sursis*, 62–63
Freud, Sigmund, 6, 7, 32, 112, 126n14
Freudian psychology, 2, 13, 28, 33, 35, 53, 104, 106, 110, 112
Fundamental project. *See* Original choice

Gallimard, Gaston (publisher), 8, 9, 39
Garaudy, Roger, 109
Gauguin, Paul, 58
Gaullist party and positions, 11, 14, 69
Gaze, 30, 33, 44, 60, 75, 76, 77
Genet, Jean, 3, 10, 14, 85, 86, *105–106*, 117

Genius, 105, 107
Gerassi, John, 16
Germans, 9, 66–67, 68, 69, 77
Germany, 7, 9, 68, 86–88, 94–97
Giacometti, Alberto, 9, 103
Gide, André, 3, 4, 6, 8, 17, 31, 37, 47, 85, 86, 103, 106, 123n8; *La Séquestrée de Poitiers,* 95
Giraudoux, Jean, 6, 90, 101; *Electre,* 74; *La Guerre de Troie n'aura pas lieu,* 131n35
Goethe, Johann Wolfgang von: *Goetz von Berlichingen,* 86
Golden Age, 120
Gratuitous act, 37
Groups. *See* Collectivities
Guillemin, Henri, 13

Haiti, 12
Hegel, Georg Wilhelm Friedrich, 5, 21, 27, 30, 112, 113, 121
Hegelian philosophy, 22
Heidegger, Martin, 7, 8, 18, *20–21,* 26, 27, 28, 33, 34, 123n9, 124n1
Hemingway, Ernest, 7, 48
Henry, O. *See* Porter, William Sydney
Heroism, 77–79
History, 41, 85, 89, 94, 96, *113–16,* 119–20
Hitler, Adolf, 8, 61, 62, 63
Holy Office, 11
Homosexuality, 43, 53, 57, 106
Howarth, William L., 107
Hugo, Victor, 2; *Hernani,* 90
Human nature, 37, 110, 120
Humanism, 28, 38, 42, 50, 99, 119
Hume, David, 21
Hungary, 14, 15, 80
Husserl, Edmund, 5, 6, 18, *19–20,* 21, 22, 23, 26, 30, 71, 101, 123n9; *Ideas,* 18
Huston, John, 16

Idealism, 5, 6, 12, 20, 22, 82, 120
Image, *21–22, 24–25,* 43, 58
Imagination, *21–22, 24–25,* 49–50
Imposture. *See* Role-playing
In-itself, *22, 26–28,* 36, 40, 75, 125n17
Inauthenticity. *See* Bad faith
Index of Forbidden Books, 11
Indochina: Roquentin in, 41; war in, 11, 14, 98
Institut Français (of Berlin), 6, 20
Instrumentality, 24
Intentionality, *21–22,* 23, 25, 26, 56, 61, 64, 114
Ionesco, Eugene, 126n5
Israel, 11, 15

James, William, 21, 24
Janet, Pierre, 24
Japan, 6, 15
Jaspers, Karl, 6, 48, 123n9
Jeanson, Francis, 8, 14, 15, 17, 108, 117, 120
Jewish question, 15, 57. *See also* Anti-Semitism; Jews
Jews, 34, 53, 57, 64, 94
John, Saint, 120
Jouvet, Louis, 86
Joyce, James, 6

Kafka, Franz, 7, 55
Kaïm, Arlette El. *See* El Kaïm, Arlette
Kant, Immanuel, 29, 111
Kantian philosophy, 19, 22
Kean, Edmund, 90
Khrushchev, Nikita, 15
Kierkegaard, Søren, 18, 20, 21, 37, 103, 124n3
Knowledge, 26, 30, 35, 42
Koestler, Arthur, 10
Korea, 12
Kosakiewicz, Olga, 7, 57

Lagache, Daniel, 24
Language, 32, 40, 45–46, 103
Lawrence, D. H., 7
Le Havre, 6, 40
Leibniz, Gottfried Wilhelm, 6, 21
Leiris, Michel, 10
Lemaître, Frédérick, 90
"Letter of 121," 15–16
Lévi-Strauss, Claude, 117
Lévy, Benny [pseud. Pierre Victor], 16
Lewis, Sinclair, 7
Libération, 16
Liberation (of Paris), 10
Limit situations, 48, 72
"Loser wins," 14, 96, 105
Love, 31–32, 43, 60, 64, 83, 96
Ludic impulse. *See* Play

McCarthyism, 12
Mallarmé, Stéphane, 103–104; *Igitur,* 103
Malraux, André, 7, 8, 72, 73, 125n18; *La Condition humaine,* 127n6, n15; *L'Espoir,* 62
Mancy, Joseph, 4–5, 54
Maoist party, 16
Marcel, Gabriel, 11
Martin du Gard, Roger, 56
Marx, Karl, 5, 6, 21, 112, 116, 121, 123n9
Marxism, 7, 12, 31, 85, 97, 100, 103, 105, 106, 109, *111–17*
Marxists. *See* Communist Party
Masochism, *32,* 45, 52, 57
Mauriac, François, 101, 106, 126n15
May 1968 student revolt, 15, 103
"Melancholia," 39
Mérimée, Prosper: "Tamango," 99
Merleau-Ponty, Maurice, 9, 10, 11, 12, 14, 103
Mescaline, 8
Metaphysical questions, 26, 36

Miller, Arthur: *The Crucible,* 84
Mitsein, 33
Montaigne, Michel de, 99
Morand, Paul, 6, 7
Munich Pact, 8, 61, 62
Music, 6, 16, 47
Musset, Alfred de: *Lorenzaccio,* 80

NRF. *See Nouvelle Revue Française*
Napoleon III (Charles-Louis-Napoléon-Bonaparte), 13
Narrative form and technique, 39, 48, 49, 50, 51, 52, *55–56,* 61–62, 65–66, 69, *70–71,* 101
Nasser, Gamal Abdel, 15
Nausea, 31, 40, 41, 44, 45
Nazi-Soviet pact, 68, 69
Need. *See* Scarcity
New Novel, 103
New York, 66, 79, 92
New York Review of Books, 16
Newtonian mechanics, 55
Nietzsche, Friedrich, 5, 18, 20, 75, 89, 104, 108, 121
Nizan, Paul, 6, 8, 68, 101, 103, 127n16
Nobel Prize, 15
North Africa, 14. *See also* Algeria
Nothingness, 25, 27, 43
Nouvelle Revue Française, 9, 101

Objectification, 30, 31, 64
Occitans, 15
Occupation (of France), 37, 56, 72, 73, 76
Olympic Games, 16
Ontological proof, 26
Ontology, 20, 21, *26–36,* 39, 46, 56
Original choice, *33–34,* 35, 104, 105–106, 107, 110
Others, 26, *30–33,* 49–50, 59–60, 64, *75–76,* 115, 116, 117

Palestine, 9
Pascal, Blaise, 18, 20, 128n10
Passion, useless, 36, 79
Past, The. *See* Time
Pathé films, 10, 83
Paz, Octavio, 120
Perception, 21–22, 24–25
Phenomenological method, 20, 23–24, 26
Phenomenological reduction, 20, 23, 30
Phenomenology, 6, 18, *19–20*, 24, 56, 70, 117
Phenomenon, definition, 26
Philosophic education in France, 5
Picasso, Pablo, 10
Plato, 112
Play, 7, 35
Poetry, 102, 103, 106
Point of view. *See* Narrative form and technique
Poland, 15
Ponge, Francis, 101
Popular Front, 7
Porter, William Sydney [pseud. O. Henry], 49
Possibility, 29, 30
Practico-inert, 115–16
Praxis, 72, 82, 104, *114–17;* definitions, 56, 114; and literature, 103
Progressive-regressive method, 110, 112
Project, *33–34,* 37, 104, 114. *See also* Original choice
Proletariat, 12, 33, 63, 73, 102, 117, 119, 120
Property, 35, 53, 93
Prose, 102, 103
Protestantism, 2, 4, 51, 88, 96, 97
Proust, Marcel, 3, 6, 48, 101, 126n5
Psychoanalysis, 13, 24, 112; existential, *35, 104,* 105, 106, 108–11. *See also* Freudian psychology

Puritanical element in Sartre's work, 2, 51

Quality, 35
Quebec separatists, 15

Racism, 15
Rassemblement Démocratique Révolutionnaire, 12
Rationalism, 18–19
Realism, 20; in the theater, 73
Realpolitik, 81
Recherches Philosophiques, 22
Relationships with others. *See* Others
Renard, Jules, 101
Resistance (underground movement), 10, 77
Responsibility, *34–35,* 37, 66, 77–78, 98, 99, 119
Ridgway, Matthew B., General, 13
Rights, 43, 44, 53, 79
Rimbaud, Arthur, 53
Robbe-Grillet, Alain, 126n9
Role-playing, 43, 52, 58, 64, 86, 91–94, 106
Romains, Jules. *See* Farigoule, Louis
roman fleuve, 56
Romantic drama, 86, 91
Rome, 14
Rotrou, Jean de, 105
Rougemont, Denis de, 101
Rousseau, Jean-Jacques, 16, 117, 120, 121
Russell War Crimes Tribunal, 16
Russia. *See* Union of Soviet Socialist Republics
Rybalka, Michel, 1, 16

Sadism, *32,* 45, 52, 57, 75–76
Saint-Exupéry, Antoine de, 7
Saint Lambert, Théaulon de, 90
Salauds, 38
Sarraute, Nathalie, 103, 126n5

Sartre, Anne-Marie. *See* Schweitzer, Anne-Marie

Sartre, Eymard, Doctor (paternal grandfather), 2

Sartre, Jean-Baptiste, 1–2, 53, 85

Sartre, Jean-Paul: childhood and youth, 1–5; early manhood, 5–9; education, 3, 4–6; family background, 1–3, 4–5; literary vocation, 3–4, 13; maturity, 9–16; military service, 6, 9; philosophical views, 6, 12–13, *18–38*, 111–18, 119–20; political views, 7–8, 10–16, 85, 103, 111–18; religious views, 4, 29, 36, 37, 89; teaching career, 6–7, 9; travels, 6–7, 10, 11–12, 14–15; wartime activities, 9–11

WORKS: CRITICISM AND BIOGRAPHY:

Baudelaire, *104–105,* 106, 107

L'Idiot de la famille, 16, *108–11,* 113

Les Mots, 2, 3, 5, 13, 16, 52, 53, 85, 97, 100, *106–108,* 110, 111

"Qu'est-ce que la littérature?" 13, *101–103*

Saint Genet, comédien et martyr, 14, *105–106,* 107, 111, 119

Situations, 16, *101–104,* 108, 119

DRAMA:

Bariona, 72, 73

Le Diable et le Bon Dieu, 14, 85, *86–90,* 97, 99, 105, 119

Huis-clos, 75–76, 94, 95, 97, 99

Kean, 14, 85, 86, *90–92,* 93

Les Mains sales, *79–82,* 86, 89, 99

Morts sans sépulture, *76–79,* 89

Les Mouches, *73–75,* 98

Nekrassov, 14, 86, *92–94*

La Putain respectueuse, 79

Les Séquestrés d'Altona, 14, 50, *94–98,* 99, 111, 115, 119

Les Troyennes, 16, *98–99*

FICTION:

L'Age de raison, *56–61,* 65

"La Chambre," *49–50,* 75, 96

Les Chemins de la liberté, 9, 11, 56 (*see also* individual volumes)

La Dernière Chance, 69

"Drôle d'amitié," *69–70*

"L'Enfance d'un chef," 8, *52–54*

"Erostrate," *50–51*

"Intimité," 51

La Mort dans l'âme, *65–69*

Le Mur, 9, 48, 70, (*see also* individual stories)

"Le Mur," 75, 78

La Nausée, 8, 9, 25, *39–48,* 56, 58, 62, 70, 100, 119

Le Sursis, *61–65,* 66, 70

FILMS:

L'Engrenage, *83–84*

Les Jeux sont faits, 83

PHILOSOPHY:

Critique de la raison dialectique, 13, 94, 97, 99, 106, 108, 109, *111–18,* 119

Esquisse d'une théorie des émotions, 8, 21, *23–24*

L'Etre et le néant, 10, 21, 22, 23, *25–36,* 40, 42, 46, 57, 63, 72, 73, 86, 104, 106, 113, 114, 116, 119

L'Existentialisme est un humanisme, 11, 18, *36–38*

L'Imaginaire, 9, 21, *24–25,* 43

L'Imagination, 8, 18, *21–22*

"La Psyché," 8

"La Transcendance de l'ego," 8, 21, *22–23*

Scarcity, 111, 114–15, 117
Schweitzer, Albert, 1
Schweitzer, Anne-Marie, 1–2, 4, 109
Schweitzer, Charles, 1–4, 107, 108
Schweitzer, Louis, 1
Schweitzer, Louise, 2, 4
Second World War, 9, 61–62,
    65–70, 80, 97, 109
Self. *See* Ego
Sequestration, 49, 75, 77, 80, 95–97
Seriality, 116–17
Sexuality, 32, 44, 50, 51, 52
Shakespeare, William, 86; *Hamlet*,
    80, 91; *Othello*, 91–92; *Romeo and
    Juliet*, 91
Sicard, Michel, 16
Simon, Claude: *La Route des Flandres*,
    65
Sincerity, 28, 86
Situation, 25, 34, 37, 72
Skiing, 35
Socialism, 7, 10, 16. *See also* Marx-
    ism; Communist Party; Socialist
    Party
Socialisme et Liberté, 10
Socialist Party, 11
Solipsism, 30
Spain, 7, 48, 116
Spanish Civil War, 8, 48, 58
Spinoza, Benedict, 6, 21
Stendhal. *See* Beyle, Henri
Surrealism, 6, 45, 53, 102
Symbolization, 24

Taine, Hippolyte, 21
Temps Modernes, Les, 11, 14, 15, 108
Théâtre Antoine, 76, 79, 80
Time, 26, *29–30,* 33, 34, 35,
    41–42, 47, 59, 65, 66, 72
Tintoretto, 16, 103
Tito, Josip Broz, Marshal, 15
Tolerance, 33
Torture, 9, 14, 16, 32, 73, 77–79,
    94, 96, 97

Totality, 113
Totalization, 113
Transcendence, *22–23, 30,* 31, 43,
    47
Treachery. *See* Treason
Treason, 67, 85, 87, 105, 117
Trojan War, 98
Trotsky, Leon, 7

Unanimists, 61
Unconscious, The, 24, 25, 28
Union of Soviet Socialist Republics,
    12, 13, 14, 15, 16, 68, 69, 70, 93,
    102
United States of America, 11, 12, 14,
    16, 102

Valéry, Paul, 6, 29, 47
Value, 27, 29, 36, 37, 43
Vécu, Le, 17, 109, 110
Venezuelan resistance, 15
Vian, Boris, 9
Vichy government, 74
Victor, Pierre. *See* Lévy, Benny
Vietnam, war in, 15, 16, 103. *See also*
    Indochina
Vietnamese refugees, 16
Vilar, Jean, 86
Violence, 73, *96–97,* 115, *119,*
    129n7
Viscous, The, *35,* 44, 60

War, *61,* 65–70, *98–99,* 115. *See also*
    individual conflicts
Will, 34
Wilson, Horace, 62
Wittgenstein, Ludwig, 6
Woolf, Virginia, 61
Working class. *See* Proletariat
World War II. *See* Second World War

Yugoslavia, 15

Zola, Emile, 61